WHO WAS
ANN GREGG?

David Cooper Holmes

P3 Publications

Dedication

Researching and writing this book, resulted in me connecting with dozens of other descendants of Ann Gregg and William Hutchinson. Following the trail, generation by generation down to living descendants led my research to Australia, New Zealand, Canada, Mexico, America, Scotland and England. Eventually I was in contact with over fifty distant cousins, all members of my new found Traveller family. The vast majority of my cousins provided their DNA for my research. It would have been impossible to solve relationships and unravel this story without this amazing joint international cooperation.
My book is dedicated to each one of them, it's their story too.

Publishing Information

David Cooper Holmes has asserted his right under the Copyright, Designs and Patents Act 1988 to be identified as the author of this work.

Copyright © David Cooper Holmes 2019

British Library Cataloguing In Publication Data
A catalogue record for this book is available from the British Library

ISBN 978-0-9931835-8-4

Published by:

P3 Publications
13 Beaver Road
Carlisle
Cumbria
CA2 7PS

Printed by:

Gomer Press Ltd
Llandysul Enterprise Park
Llandysul
Ceredigion
SA44 4JL

Index

Authors Note

The book you are about to read in only a few hours, took several years to research. The story unfolded in an extremely complex and convoluted way. I continually had to go backwards and forwards in time and place, as each person was discovered, in no particular sequence. Slowly the family connections were made and proven, making the pieces of this genealogical puzzle fit together.

To re-tell the story in a way that is less complicated and easier to follow, I have constructed the tale in a chronological sequence, starting with the oldest event, then working forward to the most recent. At times this may read a little out of sequence as it is clear that some later events were discovered before earlier ones and vice versa. However, I think this helps to give the reader a more enjoyable experience.

Preface

What began as a simple idea to research my family history, turned into an adventure that I could never have imagined.

My 5xGreat Grandmother was not what I would have expected to find.

Enigmatic from day one, trying to follow her life was almost impossible. She confused and frustrated me continually, and lived in a time and in circumstances my 21st century brain found difficult to comprehend.

She used fourteen different alias's and continually moved around the four northern counties of England.

She was incarcerated in at least seven different gaol, escaping four times.

She was a petty but serial felon, and an ancestor I should have felt ashamed of. Yet, as I got to know and understand her circumstances, and the poverty stricken life she was born into, I began to admire her strength, tenacity and ingenuity.

She was a survivor, determined to take care of her own, no matter the risk or consequence to her own life.

She was Ann Gregg.

Carlisle from Near Stanwix Bank

Chapter 1

2011 - Serious Research Began.

Like so many other people approaching retirement, I'd promised myself, that when spare time became available, I'd go back to researching my family history.

I'd researched my father's paternal line a number of years earlier, trying to find out where my double-barrelled surname came from – and succeeding. It was nothing more exciting than illegitimacy.

Now, in retirement, I started researching my father's maternal ancestors, uncovering people and stories that truly amazed me.

It began with my paternal grandmother, Elizabeth Keenan, who was born in Cockermouth in 1900. I'd known her very well, since she'd lived until I was 27.

As a child, I loved staying with her at weekends and school holidays. She lived at Seaton, in the county of Cumberland, in a detached bungalow, where she and my grandfather had something like four acres of land. My grandfather, John Holmes, had worked all his life as a railway guard. He was a very quiet, unassuming man who, in his spare time, grew fruit and vegetables and raised chickens, turkeys and geese for their table, and for sale. His special hobby was breeding singing mules – a cross between a canary and a goldfinch. I clearly remember seeing them in their show cages. Lined up on top of a privet hedge, they seemed to love the warm, spring sunshine and would sing their hearts out, while he sat and listened, his head cocked attentively to one side, carefully choosing his best singer for the next competition.

Grandad died in 1960, so from then on, whenever I stayed at Seaton, it was just me and my gran. I always liked her, even though she could be very strict. Looking back now, I can see she was very much the matriarchal type: strong, stern and dominant. But to me, she was special. She did things my friends' grandmothers never did.

She was the local Women's Institute's supreme champion at baking sponge cakes and gingerbread. Everyone was envious and wanted to know her recipes, but they were given to no-one. She fiercely guarded them as if they were worth a king's ransom. I knew her secret, but I had sworn never to tell anyone. This is the first time I have ever revealed it.

When a competition was getting close, she would take me off walking over the fields from Seaton to Siddick and Flimby. On the way, we were on the lookout for birds' nests. In particular, peewits' nests, but she would look for curlew and oyster catchers' too. This was her secret for baking. She only ever used wild birds' eggs. She reckoned they gave a special texture, richness and depth of flavour. Obviously, I would never condone this, now – it's illegal; but in those days, they were plentiful along the Solway coast and she only ever took one egg from each nest. Sometimes, if we were lucky, we found pheasant or partridge nests. Even now, I can visualise clutches of maybe twelve beautiful olive-green eggs.

We would often gather mushrooms, too. Not the supermarket button type – she taught me where to find penny buns, hedgehogs, chanterelles, morels, lawyers wigs, and others. I never knew anyone else who was interested in these varieties, although I couldn't understand why – they were delicious. She seemed to have a natural affinity with the land, but for some reason, didn't want to show it. Gran could also wring the neck of a chicken, turkey or goose without batting an eyelid, and could quickly skin and clean a rabbit or hare.

I stopped staying with her, probably around the age of thirteen or fourteen. I was simply growing up as a teenager and being with my friends took priority. At the age of sixteen, I started work and from then on, with money in my pocket for the first time, I began travelling around at weekends. I used to hitch-hike to pop concerts in the late 60s, in Bath, Buxton, Hyde Park, and the Isle of Wight. Some of my friends had moved to London, so I'd often hitch-hike to visit them.

There was a whole world to explore and experiences to be had. I was hungry to enjoy it all.

When I visited my gran and told her about all my adventures, she gave me her stern look and, wagging her finger, she said, "You've got too much gypsy blood in you! You should settle down!"

At the time, I thought that was just a typical Gran's comment: just talking metaphorically. It wasn't until years later that I realised that she meant it literally. All this seems a long time ago and it had been well and truly forgotten, until I started exploring my family history. By then, Gran was long gone. She died in 1977, leaving no stories of her past.

Starting my family research was at first a fairly simple exercise. I was just building a tree, with names, dates of birth, marriage and death; but no real details of any individual ancestor. They were just names on paper.

As my interest grew, I started digging a bit deeper, becoming interested in my ancestors' occupations. I noticed that my gran's father, Daniel Keenan, was shown on the 1891 census as living with his parents on Sullart Street in Cockermouth, working as a warehouseman. On the 1901 census he was a pot hawker, and by 1911 he was a general dealer and licensed hawker.

Daniel's father was John Keenan, born in 1835 in County Down, Ireland. He first appeared on the 1851 census, where his occupation was collier, by 1861, he had become a labourer – perfectly normal occupations for a poor Irishman who had fled Ireland with his parents to escape the potato famine. In 1859, John married Elizabeth McKenzie, and his life seemed to take a change, after this.

Although the 1861 census shows him living at Dearham and working as a labourer, the census also shows that he was living next door to his brother-in-law, Charles McKenzie, and his father-in-law, John McKenzie, who were both earthenware dealers. The next census in 1871 showed John as a hawker, so I'm guessing he was hawking pots, like his in-laws. 1881 shows him as a costermonger and hawker. A quick search of old occupations revealed that a costermonger was "a person who sells goods, especially fruit and vegetables, from a handcart in the street". By the time of the 1891 census, his occupation is "General Dealer", and someone added the word "shop" to the description. The final census in which John appeared was in 1901, where he is described as a "Glass, China and Earthenware Dealer". This was clearly showing the pattern of a developing enterprise. After searching through local trade directories, I found the most surprising entry for John – he was shown as a "Marine Store Dealer", which surprised me, because Cockermouth is eight miles from the sea.

When I searched for the definition of a "Marine Store Dealer," the answer really surprised me: "a junk dealer in scrap materials, the type of work often done by gypsies". The description said that they "operated at the hub of a barter economy in crockery, fur, wool, rabbit skins, and anything of value". So much for being eight miles from the sea! Marine Store Dealers had nothing to do with boats.

So, was my ancestor, John Keenan, a Gypsy or a Traveller?

There were several different groups of Travelling families in Britain in those days, including Romany Gypsies, Roma, Irish Travellers and New Travellers. There were also Circus and Fairground families who could belong to any group. Some cultural values and traditions were shared by them all, including a nomadic lifestyle.

Gypsies are Romany ethnic groups whose ancestors migrated from India from the 10th Century, and then mixed with European and other groups. 'Roma' is used to describe European Romany-speaking groups who have come to England from Eastern and Central Europe, and the word is sometimes used to refer more generally to Gypsies and Travellers. Irish Travellers are a nomadic group with a distinctive way of life, who have been part of Irish society for centuries. New Travellers are people from a settled background who, through circumstance or necessity, took to a travelling lifestyle as a way of earning a living.

I have never been able to find any history on John Keenan, his family, or anything of their life in Ireland; although through DNA comparisons, I believe I have discovered two of his father's siblings. One family followed a normal working-class lifestyle; the other family had a military background. All this suggests that John Keenan was the first to become involved with the Travelling community, and therefore a New Traveller.

It was fairly clear to me that he had learned the earthenware trade from his wife's family, and being a natural entrepreneur, he had added to and developed his business skills, seeking a better life. I could find no evidence of him travelling with his wares, as a traditional Traveller would have done, but I'm sure he hawked his goods around all the villages between Maryport and Cockermouth.

Going back to my family tree, I followed the branch of my grandmother Elizabeth Keenan's maternal line. Her mother was Annie Knowles, born in 1880 in Greysouthern, near Cockermouth. Annie's father was Richard Knowles, who had been born at Kendal. It didn't take much searching to find that they came from a huge family of Knowles, spread all over Cumberland, Westmorland, North Lancashire and North Yorkshire – and almost all were potters, pot hawkers or earthenware dealers. So, this was my grandmother's maternal family. I quickly learned that the Knowles were a typical Travelling family. The big give-away was that their children were all baptised in different places, as was common for people travelling around.

Annie Knowles mother was Annie Berry from Penrith, whose family were mainly besom (hazel-twig broom) makers or basket makers – another traditional occupation of Gypsies or Travellers. Annie's father, Thomas Berry, had married a Martha Hutchinson. I found Thomas, Martha and their family on the 1861 census, living in tents. The address given was "Rowan tree", Lynesack and Softley, County Durham. The rowan tree is mentioned because it's a fixed point, the nearest identifier to mark the location of their encampment.

There is a romantic notion that Travellers and Gypsies roamed through a beautiful, warm, sunny countryside full of wild flowers and butterflies, in their gaily painted Gypsy caravans. In fact, nothing could be further from the truth. Gypsy caravans or, more correctly, "vardo's" didn't come into existence until around the mid-1850s, And then, only the wealthiest Travellers could afford them. They didn't become commonplace amongst the Travelling community until the turn of the twentieth century. Instead, Thomas and Martha would have made an encampment by building a bender tent. This involved cutting long lengths of willow, ash or hazel, inserting them into the ground in two opposite straight lines about two metres apart at roughly 50 cm intervals, then bending the lengths of wood over and tying the opposite sides together at the top, to form an overturned boat shape. Next, overlapping blankets, felt, or waterproof sheets were laid over the framework and pinned onto the frame. If the Travellers were planning to set up camp and stay for a while, they would build a more open style of tent called a "balk" at one end of the main tent. This protected the entrance against the weather and was the place to build a fire, for cooking and warmth. If a large family group were setting up camp for the winter, they would often join several bender tents at the balk. It would have been a tough life. Travelling with all your possessions. Heaving them in and out of carts. Stopping and setting up camp wherever you could find people to buy what you made or traded, and where you weren't hounded out or forced to get off the land. Often facing racism and suspicion. A life of makeshift homes and a rootless existence. Life was certainly not romantic, by any means.

Thomas and his family had probably had enough of this lifestyle, and with the promise of a new life, they emigrated to America in 1892. Martha, along with two of her sisters, appears on the 1900 USA census which shows their occupations to be "fortune tellers". Was this another clue to my link to Gypsies?

I had gone back in time, following that particular branch of my tree, to my 4-times great grandparents, John Berry, and his wife, Ann. The earliest record of their names I had been able to find was the baptism of their first child, Jane, at St Michael's Church, Torpenhow, Cumberland, in 1830. Following this, came the baptisms of Mary, Hugh, Ann and finally, Thomas, who had been baptised at Barton, Westmorland in 1836. All the baptism records show John's occupation as besom maker or basket maker.

My family was full of Travellers and Gypsies and I had known absolutely nothing about it! All of a sudden, it dawned on me: I now knew where my Grandmother's special skills came from. Telling me I had too much gypsy blood! It was all true. Fascinated, I wanted to know more.

I couldn't get any further backwards in time with that particular family, so I went sideways, on to different branches of my family tree. Returning to my 2-times great grandfather, John Keenan, I looked into his wife, Elizabeth McKenzie. I found that her father, John McKenzie, was a potter and her grandfather, another John, was a razor grinder in Carlisle. Again, these were classic occupations for Travellers. Already, I'd discovered that a quarter of my family tree were Travelling folk, and I wanted to know each one of them better.

I spent months reading about Travellers and Gypsies, their history, culture and lifestyle, trying to understand more about my ancestors and their place in social history. I learned to follow my family's travels by using the baptismal records of their children. This showed the routes they followed, as they were selling their wares. Travellers were clearly habitual, following the same routes to seasonal markets and fairs. Some journeys went from West Cumbria, via Wigton, Holme Abbey and Carlisle, into south-west Scotland. Others went from Cockermouth via Penrith and Brough, to Durham. There were other routes, too – around Westmorland, Lancashire and North Yorkshire.

The pattern of travel clearly showed that many of them descended on the same place in early June, most years: Appleby Horse Fair. Said to be the largest traditional horse fair of its kind in the world.

Appleby Horse Fair was set up by charter under the Reign of King James II in 1685, and it has been an annual event ever since. Originally, it was a venue for trading all kinds of livestock and general merchandise. But its popularity with the large number of Gypsies who came each year eventually led to the fair becoming a specialist horse fair.

All the family research I had done so far was by using conventional methods – census and parish records. To get further back and to add depth to the characters,

I needed to start researching old newspapers, go to the county archives and take a DNA test.

This eventually led me to my 5-times great grandmother, Ann Gregg.

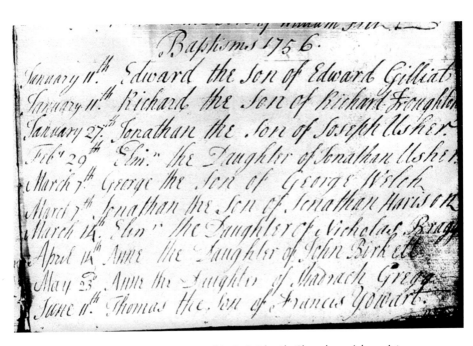

Ann Gregg's Baptism Record in St Bridget's Church parish register

Chapter 2
1756 - Ann Gregg

Ann Gregg was baptised in St Bridget's Church, Moresby, Cumberland, England, on 23rd May, 1756. At the time of her birth, her parents were staying at Wigton, Cumberland. Ann's uncle Henry was staying at Scilly banks, Moresby, so Ann's family were more than likely staying with Henry, hawking their wares in the Whitehaven area, when Ann came into the world.

Ann's father, Shadrach Gregg, was a travelling tinker, his place of settlement was Nichol Forest, Cumberland – the most northerly parish in England.

The Greggs had descended from the ancient Scottish tribe of Picts, who had inhabited and defended their lands along the Scotland-England border for centuries.

The Romans called them the Picti, "those with painted or tattooed bodies", and they were renowned as fearless fighters. In AD 122, the Roman Emperor Hadrian gave instructions to build a wall from Maia (Bowness on Solway) to Segedunum (Wallsend), a distance of approximately seventy-three miles from the west coast to the east. Rome had already conquered England, but had failed to bring Scotland under its rule. The reason for this was the Picts, who frequently raided the Roman territory using guerrilla-style tactics, stealing cattle and capturing slaves. These constant raids took their toll on Rome's westernmost frontier, to the point that Hadrian thought the only solution was a to build a wall to keep them out. Three hundred years later, Rome abandoned the wall – and Britain. The Picts, however, remained. Over the next few centuries, they fought continual battles to protect their lands from the Angles.

Stewart Mowatt, Vice President of the Pictish Arts Society wrote:

> *Battles over land and dominance often erupted between the Picts and the diverse peoples with whom they lived in uneasy proximity. By the 7th century, the Angles posed the biggest threat to the Picts. For some time, the Northumbrian's had been flexing their muscles in an effort to expand their kingdom to the west and north. To the Picts' anger, they now controlled much of the land as far north as the Firth of Tay. Following the death of the Anglian King Oswui, the Picts rebelled, but the consequences were nothing short of disastrous. The new Anglian King, Ecgfrith, and his army met the Pictish forces on the southern side of the Firth of Forth in 672AD and a bloody battle ensued. It is said that so many Picts died it was possible to walk across the bodies in the Rivers Carron and Avon without getting wet. The Picts needed a new strategy*

if they were to avoid further oppression and it came in the form of a new Pictish king, Bridei, son of Bili. It would not be long before he would be put to the test in a defining moment in Scottish history.

On May 20, 685AD, Ecgfrith, against the advice of his friends, councillors and his newly appointed bishop, led his army into Pictish territory. They stumbled across a Pictish war party that turned and fled and the Northumbrian army gave chase. Sensing first blood, Ecgfrith pursued the Picts into the paths of inaccessible mountains near to a place called Dún Nechtain. By the time he realised his mistake, it was too late. The trap was sprung and hordes of Pictish warriors emerged to slay Ecgfrith and his army.

The exact location of the battle is debated but it was to change the course of history. The Picts wasted no time in recovering all the land lost over many decades to the Northumbrian's and, around the same time, the first references to Pictland or Pictavia emerge.

This was the Greggs' heritage – their strength of character, fierce protectiveness and determination to survive were firmly embedded in their genes.

Hadrian's wall was only a few miles from Nichol Forest, and it must have featured regularly in the Greggs' lives. The Military Way, a road built by the Romans, was the main route from Carlisle to Newcastle, and this would have been used regularly by the Greggs as they travelled between the west and east of northern England.

When they weren't travelling, the Gregg family lived at Bakeston Gill. They had spent their winters here for at least three generations. They were classed as cottagers, which was someone who leased a plot of land with a small cottage on it. It was said that a Cumberland clay cottager's house could be built by a family in three or four hours, so it was fairly basic. The land was usually worked by the family to grow vegetables, and it may have had a pig pen for small livestock.

Bakeston Gill comprised of two cottages: one occupied by Shadrach Gregg, Ann's father; the other by her uncle, Henry. Their homes were about as basic as you can imagine: cobblestone and clay walls, a compacted earth floor and a turf roof.

There were no windows in the cottage, only a front door into the single room where the whole family lived, ate and slept. A peat or wood fire was built on the floor in the middle of the room, but there was no chimney, so smoke filled the room, seeping out gradually through the turf roof. The whole family lived here through the bleak, bitterly cold northern British winter months. During the better months, from April to October, they travelled, selling their wares at markets and fairs. In the travelling season, the family lived in their bender tent, which could be put up or taken down in less than an hour. Sometimes, they would rent a cottage for the summer months in the area where business and opportunities were good.

The River Liddle marked the parish boundary of Nichol Forest, as well as the border between Scotland and England, and the river bank was less than twenty paces from Bakeston Gill cottages. This all made it an ideal place to live for anyone who needed to avoid the authorities on either side of the border.

It has to be said that Ann Gregg, even as an innocent baby, was born into a rough, tough, criminal family. At the time of Ann's baptism, both her great Aunt, Jane Gregg, and Jane's daughter who was known to the authorities as "Jane Gregg the younger", were in hiding. They had been transported to the plantations and colonies of the Americas in 1752, onboard the convict ship, Lichfield. A local newspaper had reported:

The Newcastle Courant on 7th March 1752

This day se'nnight the Shop of Mr George Young, Shoe maker in the Middle street, was broken open, when thirty pairs of shoes and two pairs of boots were stole and the Robbers got away undiscovered.

The night following, the shop of Mr Philipson was attempted to be broken open, but it being too secure for the villains, they were obliged to make off without any booty.

We are desired to acquaint the publick that John Fall, Ann Fall, Jane Greg, Margaret Fall, John Anderson, James Robertson, William Fall, Elizabeth Taylor, Robert Clark, and Elizabeth his wife, Jane Greg, Jane Campbell, Robert Gibson, and Peter Brown, Part of the Gang of Faws, which has so long infested this County, are now confined in Morpeth gaol, on suspicion of divers felonies and misdemeanours, where it is hoped and desired that all persons who have been robb'd or hurt by that dangerous set of people, will go and view them, in order to their being convicted, and properly punished.

"Faws" was local slang for a group of itinerant tinkers, besom makers, muggers and such like. The word derives from John Faa, a strolling gypsy, said to be the King of all Scottish Gypsies in the mid-16th century.

The two Gregg women were transported with other members of the Gang of Faws, a notorious local gang of petty felons. Somehow, they escaped in 1754, returning to England, and were on the run, hiding along the Borders. There was a reward of £5 if any member of the gang were apprehended. Descriptions of the gang members said they were swarthy and gypsy-like in appearance.

Newcastle Courant 27th July 1754

NORTHUMBERLAND Whereas Robert Armstrong, John Fall, and Margaret his wife, William Fall, and Jane, otherwise Ann his wife, Robert Clarke and Isabel his wife, Thomas Kimmins, Peter otherwise Charles Brown, Jane Gregg the elder, Jane Gregg the younger, Elizabeth Clarke, James Cowburn, otherwise Cockburn and Dominic MacConnell (commonly called or known by the name of Faws, being severally convicted of petty Larceny and other Crimes by them severally committed, within the Benefit of the Statute, were on or about the 15th day of April 1752, transported to some of his Majesties Colonies and Plantations in America, for the term of seven years, from which they have severally returned, and are now wandering or lurking within some part of the said County. Notice therefore is hereby given, that if any person shall apprehend the said several offenders, or any of them, and convey them, or any of them before anyone or more of his Majesties Justices of the Peace for the said County, so as he, she, or they may be committed to the Gaol of the said County, the person or persons so apprehending and conveying the said offenders, or any of them, before one or more Justice or Justices of the Peace as aforesaid, shall for every person so by him apprehended and conveyed, have paid for him, or them, by the Treasurer of the said County, a reward of five Pounds.

N.B. The said Robert Armstrong is about 37 years of Age, five foot and six inches high, strong made, and of swarthy complexion like a Gipsy.

The said John Fall is about 30 Years of Age, five foot nine inches high, and of swarthy complexion. His wife Margaret is pretty tall, has several freckles on her face, and red hair.

The said William Fall is about twenty seven years of age, five foot ten inches high, and of swarthy complexion, and Jane, otherwise Ann his wife, is a short, strong made woman and marked with the small-pox.

The said Robert Clarke is about 35 years of age, five foot seven inches high, and marked with small-pox, and Isabel, his Wife is of a fair complexion, thin made and has black hair.

The said Thomas Kimmins is about 26 years of age, five foot seven inches high, thin made and of a brown complexion.

The said Peter otherwise Charles Brown is about 17 years of Age, of a fair complexion, and has a round Face.

The said Jane Gregg the Elder, is about 46 years of Age, low in stature, gross made, and of a swarthy complexion.

The said Jane Gregg the Younger, is about 20 years of Age, of fair complexion, and marked with the small-pox.

The said Elizabeth Clarke is about 22 years of Age, of swarthy complexion, and has black hair.

The said James Cowburn, otherwise Cockburn, is about 40 years of Age, five foot five inches high, is an able bodied Man, has black curl'd Hair, is marked with the small-pox, and of a swarthy complexion.

The said Dominic MacConnell is about 50 years of Age, five foot five inches high, the Hairs both of his Head and Beard are Grey, his Head shakes as if affected by the Palsey, and he appears to be lame in one of his hands.

By the order of the Court of Sessions. DENTON

Convicts escaping from transportation to the American colonies and making their way back to England wasn't as unusual or rare an occurrence as you might think – particularly for members of established gangs.

Convicts belonging to criminal gangs were more likely than individuals to return to England from America, because their gangs provided a support system for any member caught by the authorities. Even before it came to court, gangs had a ready-made list of false witnesses who could provide alibis for any member who was caught and brought to trial. If that member was still found guilty and sentenced to transportation, the gang provided money for the convict to purchase privileges onboard the ship or once the ship landed, to buy their freedom and a trip back to England.

In his best-selling book, *The Discoveries of John Poulter alias Baxter*, published in 1754, John Poulter gives a full account of his criminal career and exposes the common practices of criminals.

He describes the method by which convicts returned from transportation:

> *"After they are in a Part of North America, the general Way is this, just before they go on board a Ship, their Friend or Accomplices purchase them their Freedom from the Merchant or Captain that belongs to the said Ship, for about ten Pound Sterling, some gives more and some less; then the Friend of the Convict or Convicts get a Note from the Merchant, or Captain, that the Person is free to go unmolested, when the Ships arrive between the Capes of Virginia, where they please."*

Once the convicts had secured their freedom, Poulter continues, they then looked for a ship that would take them back to England. Again, for a fee provided by their criminal network.

Convicts almost never returned on the same ship that took them to America. The risk of taking a convict back across the Atlantic would have been too great for the convict merchants. The British government prohibited them from helping any convict return to England, and if they were ever caught doing so, it would have jeopardised their highly profitable business. There were plenty of other ships, however, willing to take paying passengers back to England. Convicts who didn't have enough money would look for opportunities to work onboard the ship as compensation for their passage.

If convicts could not secure their freedom upon arrival, Poulter says, they would run away from their master, and *"lay in the Woods by Day, and travel by Night for Philadelphia, New York, or Boston, in which Place no Questions are asked them."*

Poulter goes on to claim that the ease with which convicts could return from transportation

> *"encourages a great many to commit Robberies more than they would, because they say they do not mind Transportation, it being but four or five Months pleasure, for they can get their Freedom and come home again."*

At his trial, the transported convict Bampfylde-Moore Carew expressed the kind of nonchalant attitude towards transportation that Poulter declares to be typical. After the judge passed a sentence of transportation and told Carew that he would now *"proceed to a hotter climate,"* the convict enquired, "What climate?"

> *"... and being told Merryland, he with great Composure made a critical Observation on the Pronunciation of that Word, implying that he apprehended it ought to be pronounced 'Maryland', and added, it would save him Five Pounds for his Passage, as he was very desirous of seeing that Country."*

Carew later escaped just as he was being sold to some planters, but he was eventually caught. As punishment, the captain had him flogged with a cat o' nine tails and secured an iron collar around his neck to prevent him from escaping again.

Poulter concludes his section on convict transportation by offering an unwieldy bureaucratic solution to the problem of returning convicts. First, he recommends fining any merchant or captain who frees a convict upon arrival. Then he proposes that anyone bound homeward on a ship should be required to publicly publish his or her name and intent to travel abroad, and that person should then secure a certificate from the governor stating that he or she is not an indentured servant or a convict. These steps, he proclaims, *"would prevent such a Number of Convicts coming back again before their Time is expired."*

Any convict escaping and returning to England, automatically received the death penalty. A substantial reward was offered to anyone identifying an escaped convict, leading to their capture. It isn't difficult to imagine the dangers of being on the run.

The two Jane Greggs must have used gang money to secure their release and passage home – as evidenced by the sheer number of their gang members who returned, all at the same time. Clearly, transportation to America was not a deterrent and nor was the possible death penalty they faced on their return.

Ann Gregg's Uncle Henry seemed to be a gang member too, although at this stage it's not clear whether he was with the Gang of Faws. There are Clarks' associated with the Gang of Faws and Clarks' reported here with Henry Gregg. Is this just a coincidence ?

The following Felons are to take their Trials at the Assizes for the City of Carlisle, which began this Day, viz. William Grieve the Elder, charged with Murder, John and Dorothy Bodle, charged with Cow-stealing, Isaac Robinson, Christopher Hall, William Ladlow, Henry Gregg, David Miller, John and William Clarke, charged with house breaking. John Glasby, for intermarrying with Jane Selby, his former Wife being still living; William Forrester, William Nixon.

Documents discovered in the National Archives in London gave more of an insight into their alleged crimes. The examination of Henry Gregg on 26th March 1758 stated :-

The examinant being charged with a felony upon the warehouses of Younger and Wilkinson last night, sayeth that he was last night about Eight o'Clock at the house of William Clark at Scilly banks and then went to his own house at 12 o'Clock at night he called up John Crosby's wife to come to his house, his wife being in labour, and that he did not leave his house or the neighbourhood all night and went to bed about 3 or 4 o'Clock in the morning, that between 12 o'Clock when he called up John Crosby's wife till 3 o'Clock he went to John Crosby's house to see what o'Clock it was and spoke to John Crosby and that he was never out of his own house for quarter of an hour together during that time and further sayeth nothing.

There seemed to be some truth in Henry's statement. Moresby parish records show the baptism of his daughter Ann only one week later, on April 2nd 1758.

The evidence given by John Rudock seemed to be more damning.

This informant sayeth that one day in the week before Easter Sunday last, One Henry Gregg of Scilly Banks came to this informants house and asked him to buy some tobacco which he agreeing to, the said Gregg carried him to his own house and sold him thirty three pounds weight of tobacco at four pence halfpenny a pound, which this informant Paid him the said Gregg twelve shillings and fourpence halfpenny for it, and

*he said Gregg told him that he expected more of such sort of tobacco,
or words to that sense and he this informant agreed to give him the
same price for what tobacco he should get of the same goodness, and
the informant sayeth that he looked upon the tobacco delivered him by
Gregg to be very good and of much better quality than common.*

This wasn't looking good for Henry. A quick internet search and I'd learned that
Younger and Wilkinson who owned the warehouse, were tobacco merchants.
The next examination of John Clark gave more insight into the events on the
evening in question.

*The informant upon oath sayeth, that Henry Gregg and William Lindsay
and one Wilson came to William Clarks house at Scilly banks after
sunset yester night where the informant was, and they desired his
father and him to go down to Whitehaven with sacks and that they
would get some goods, that they might make a penny on which they
consented to, and they remained in his fathers house till about twelve
o'Clock at night, when they set forward for Whitehaven, that is to say
Henry Gregg, William Lindsay and Wilson, his father William Clarke and
himself and they came together to the houses in Bransty Ropewalk.
Henry Gregg then bid this informant and his father William Clark they
stand in the road near the houses to watch whether anybody was
coming, and said Gregg, Lindsay and Wilson went up amongst the
houses and in a little time he heard a pistol go off and the said Gregg
Wilson and Lindsay came from amongst these houses and ran away
and he this informant was sayeth that his father, Gregg, Wilson and
Lindsay had sacks with them, which was to bring of the goods that
Henry Gregg told them of which they were to get.*

This informants examination was clearly showing that Henry Gregg was the
leader of the gang and making all the decisions. "Pistol go off", this sounded
like a much more serious event to me. The examination didn't make clear who's
pistol went off. Were Henry and his gang doing the shooting or being shot at.
In my imagination it was Henry and gang being shot at by warehouse guards.

There were several other examinations before the assizes took place, but they revealed
nothing new to add to the story. Until the final examination of William Clark.

The information of William Clark of Sillybanks taken on Oath before me this 27th of March 1758

This informant on Oath sayth, That about a month since Henry Gregg of Sillybanks told him that he had a parcell of Tobacco to send to his Brother Shadrach Gregg and desired him to carry it at Wigton, and that he woud pay him for his Trouble, to which he consented, and about three weeks Since he delivered him this informant a parcell of loose leaf Tobacco, about four stone or fifty six pounds which he carryed upon his Galloway, and accordingly he delivered the said Tobacco to Shadrach Gregg who carryed it to one Charles Steward a potter and he received money for it, and Shadrach Gregg gave this informant three shillings and Six pence for the carriage — That on Saturday night about sunsett Henry Gregg and one Lindsey and some more men that he did not well know, came to buy informants house, and that Henry Gregg desired him and his son John Clark to go down that night to Whitehaven with him and bid them take sacks with them and that he coud get some goods, that a penny might be made off, which they consented to, and about midnight they sett forward, Henry Gregg himself & son John Clark, Lindsey, and another he did not know, and came by the head of Brausty Gill cross the fields to the houses near the ropewalk at Brausty, and then Henry Gregg bid him and his son stand watch to see if any body came, then Gregg and the other two went up among the houses, and after some time they came running out from among the houses, a pistoll fired, and they run away, and he was taken —

Sworn this 27th March 1758
Before Peter How

William Clark

Henry Gregg Steals Tobacco - Examination of William Clark

21

This informant on oath sayeth, that about a month since Henry Gregg of Scilly banks told him that he had a parcel of tobacco to send to his brother Shadrach Gregg at Wigton and desired him to carry it and he would pay him for his trouble, to which he consented and about three weeks since he delivered him this informant a parcel of loose tobacco about four stones or fifty six pounds which he carried upon his Galloway, (A Galloway was a type of pony native to the Border counties, now extinct. It was said to be good looking with a deep chest, making it an ideal pack horse in rough country) *and accordingly he delivered the said tobacco to Shadrach Gregg who carried it to on Charles Steward a potter and he received money for it and Shadrach Gregg gave him the informant three shillings and sixpence for the carriage. - That on Saturday night last, about sunset, Henry Gregg and Lindsay and some more men that he did not well know, came to this informants house and that Henry Gregg desired him and his son John Clark to go down that night to Whitehaven with him and bid them take sacks with them and that he could get some goods that a penny might be made of, which they consented to and about midnight they set forward Henry Gregg, himself and son John Clark, Lindsay and another he did not know and came by the head of Bransty Gill cross the fields to the houses near the Ropewalk at Bransty and then Henry Gregg bid him and his son stand watch to see if anybody came. Then Gregg and the other two went up amongst the houses and after some they can running out from amongst the houses a pistol fired and they ran away and he was taken.*

So, it looks like stealing tobacco was a regular occurrence, and that Henry's brother Shadrach (Ann Gregg's father) was complicit in the crimes, as he was distributing stolen goods. I searched local newspapers for details of the court case. All I have been able to find is a very small report dated August 12th 1758 stating that Henry Gregg, William Clark and John Clark were acquitted. No mention is made of Lindsay or Wilson. It's difficult to understand how Henry was acquitted after reading all the evidence against him in the examinations. Without being able to find the indictment and court records we'll never know what other evidence was presented to the court.

No other reports of Henry's criminal activities were found until fifteen years later :-

At the Assize, William Elliott, for returning from transportation, received sentence of death. Henry Gregg, Charles Campbell and Hugh Stuart for shop breaking, and Eleanor Campbell and Mary Graham for theft, to be transported seven years.

Henry was transported to America onboard the Tayloe, under the captaincy of John Ogilvie. The Tayloe was carrying 94 convicts from London to Virginia.

One morning Ogilvie spotted an extraordinarily beautiful bird sitting on the bowsprit. As soon as he saw the bird he called for his gun and shot it. His aim wasn't perfect and the bird fluttered for a while before it fell dead into the ocean. Undeterred from his desire to posses the bird, Ogilvie called out to the convicts that "which ever of them could get the bird for him, would immediately be given his freedom. Several convicts stripped off their clothes, dived in and raced for the bird. Just as the first convict arrived at the floating bird and reached out to grab it, a shark rose from the depths and bit off his other are. Desperate for the promise of freedom, and with the bird in tow, he struggled back to the ship using his remaining arm. The crewe hauled the prisoner from the water and it was delivered to the captain. `the prisoner then died on the spot.

Later in the voyage as the Tayloe headed for shore in Chesapeake Bay, lightning struck the ship destroying the mast and stunning all onboard. Fortunately no-one was killed.

Whether or not Henry was the swimmer, or he arrived, worked out his seven years, or escaped, managing to return to England I don't know.

I wondered what it must be like to be transported to the colonies at that time, doing some research gave me a vivid picture. It wasn't a pretty one. Conditions on convict ships bound for the Americas were harsh. The "transports" spent almost the entire eight to ten-week voyage below the decks, in cramped quarters, chained together in groups of five or six.

Convict ships in general were not large. Most of those used in this trade were built in America, mainly in Maryland and New England where there was an abundance of wood suitable for shipbuilding. The rest were constructed in

Britain, with a very smaller percentage having been seized from the French as booty during wartime. The ships tended to be old and well-worn from their frequent trips back and forth across the Atlantic. Their rotting hulks often required costly repairs that cut deep into the profits of the convict contractors.

Even though custom-built slave ships were sometimes employed to transport prisoners, most of the ships used in the transportation business were for trading goods and were ill-equipped to handle the movement of human cargo. Many of them were better suited to their other role: carrying tobacco and other commodities back across the Atlantic from the colonies, once the convicts had been unloaded in America. There was no sense in sailing an empty vessel back, and not enough paying passengers to cover costs. Cargo's of rum from the Caribbean and Tobacco from America could be very lucrative.

Sailors and gaolers often referred to the people sentenced to transportation as being sent or sold 'into slavery'. The comparison is apt, since convicts were generally given to ships' captains in return for them transporting the prisoners for a very low fee. The captains made their money by selling the convicts into labour when they arrived in America.

There were other similarities, in the conditions under which both convicts and slaves were carried across the Atlantic. Both were human cargo, and in fact, many of the contractors, captains, and ships in the convict trade had also worked in the slave trade.

Even though merchants in both the convict and slave trades had a financial incentive to keep their passengers healthy – to a degree, convicts were treated worse than slaves. Slave traders only profited from the sale of their human cargo at the end of the voyage. Slaves commanded much higher prices than convicts, as a convict would be released after their term of sentence. Hence there was more incentive to deliver slaves in as healthy a state as possible. Since the convict trader was already receiving a subsidy from the British government for each convict transported, there was more temptation to cut corners or reduce basic provisions to the convicts, so as to increase their profits.

A letter from the Earl of Fife to George Selwyn on April 28, 1770, gives a snapshot of the conditions under which convicts were transported.

"I went on board, and, to be sure, all the states of horror I ever had an idea of are much short of what I saw this poor man in; chained to a board, in a hole not above sixteen feet long; more than fifty with him;

a collar and padlock about his neck, and chained to five of the most dreadful creatures I ever looked on".

The prospect of this fate should have been an immense deterrent, yet the Greggs clearly had no fear of the law, nor of its consequences. In their desperately poor situation, food and simple survival came before anything else.

Traveling families like the Greggs lived on the edge of society and had regular brushes with the law. Consequently there are many historical records available, describing the lives of this community. Old newspapers give descriptions of offences such as petty theft, poaching, vagrancy etc. Archived documents such as indictments, petitions and prosecutions give even more details. Looking at the conditions of the poor at that time, and their desperate situation, it is easy to understand why so many were forced into a life of petty crime.

The second half of the 18th century saw immense changes throughout Britain. The industrial revolution was transforming life, and what had predominantly been a rural society was becoming more urban. The population were migrating towards towns and cities, seeking employment in mills, mines and factories.

Improved transport links, like the completion of the main road to Newcastle and the increase of turnpike roads, enabled Carlisle to share in the benefits of Britain's industrial revolution – and its drawbacks.

In 1763, a survey conducted at the request of the Bishop of Carlisle, Charles Lyttelton, found the population of Carlisle to be 4,158. In 1780, another survey conducted under the direction of Dr John Heysham found that the city's inhabitants had increased to 7,677. This population explosion was a result of the rapid growth of industrialisation in the city, particularly in new areas just outside the city walls. This growing industrial base revolved around water-powered textile mills that specialised in finishing linen and cloth. Calico printing began in 1761 and gingham check and bleaching businesses followed shortly after. Carlisle's importance as a manufacturing town was firmly established when a large woollen mill was set up by a group of Hamburg merchants. Tanners, brewers and hat makers all added to the industrial mix. Everything looked as if it was going well, and it was – for the upper classes.

Owning land was the main form of wealth at that time. Power and influence were in the hands of rich landowners. At the top of the social hierarchy were the aristocrats and nobility; below them were the gentry. A diminishing class in the 18th century was the yeomanry, who worked small parcels of land they owned, and were positioned between the rich and the poor. The greatest mass of the population was poor and uneducated. And at the absolute bottom of the heap were the Travellers.

Living as cottagers, the Greggs had the use of a small parcel of land around their cottage. This could have been supplemented by using common land and, perhaps, some rough marginal land, where wood for their fire could be gathered. But the Land Enclosures Act was putting a stop to all this.

Although the Act had been in existence for many years beforehand, agricultural prices in the first half of the 18th century had been stagnant. This had given the elite no incentive to petition Parliament for enclosure rights, since there was no money to be made from the land.

The process to achieve an enclosure was ponderous. It involved petitioning to present a bill, then putting the bill to the house, and appointing commissioners to oversee the enclosure. This was an expensive and time-consuming process, but one that usually passed with very little attention to detail, since both Houses of Parliament were full of landowners and their place-men. If the landowners wanted it, the landowners made the decision to approve it. But few petitions of that nature were received while agricultural land was of little value. Such an expensive process to enclose land that yielded low returns didn't make economic sense. Until things changed.

During the period 1700 – 1760, only 152 petitions were received by Parliament, to enclose 300,000 acres. From 1761 – 1800, 2000 petitions were acted on, enclosing 3.1 million acres.

With a growing demand for additional roads, factories, houses and town and city infrastructures arising from the industrial revolution, land was suddenly seen as potentially far more valuable. Instead of letting their land lie unused or open for common public use, landowners saw that it could be increasingly valuable and in demand, for sale, rental, development or use. They needed to stake their claim of ownership.

Now that there was a rush to enclose land, the results, as usual, hit the poorest people the hardest.

An anonymous poem of the time, goes:

> They hang the man and flog the woman
> That steals the goose from off the common
> But let the greater villain loose
> That steals the common from the goose.

Great changes were occurring in trade in Carlisle, and by the third quarter of the 18th century, industry consisted almost entirely of the manufacture of cotton goods, which now took place on a massive scale.

There were around 1,200 hand looms working in the city, and even more in the surrounding towns and villages. To satisfy the huge appetite for cotton yarn to weave, there were eleven cotton mills in town, utilising 80,000 spindles.

But things were changing rapidly with increasing mechanisation as the industrial age developed. And as the rich got comfortably richer, the poor became significantly poorer.

Edmund Cartwright, a clergyman, had invented the power loom. After visiting the newly-mechanised cotton-spinning mills owned by his friend, Richard Arkwright, Cartwright recognised that with cotton being spun at such an industrial rate, to keep pace, the finished yarn would have to be exported, as England just didn't have enough capacity, with its hand-loom weaving to consume the finished yarn. He became determined to bring the same level of mechanisation to weaving as had already been brought to spinning. Although he failed in his own business venture, his designs worked. Cartwright continued the development of power looms until the process was automated.

The change from labour-intensive manual manufacturing to automated mechanisation put hundreds of Carlisle citizens out of work. At the peak of hand-loom weaving, somewhere between 20% and 25% of the population of the city and its surrounds had been employed in hand-loom weaving. This dramatic collapse in employment brought unimaginable poverty and despair.

This was the life and time into which Ann Gregg was born.

Cumberland to wit The Information of Mary Furnas of Wigton in the said County _____ taken on Oath Before me Thomas Wilson Doctor in Divinity _____ an oath one of his Majestys Justices of the peace in & for the said County this 15th day of February 1777

This Informant saith that yesterday in the Evening about six oClock she was sitting in our back Shop or apartment in Wigton afd when on hearing the Tinkle of the Bell at the Front Shop door she this Informant immediately went into her said Front Shop & saw a woman standing with the door about half shut in her hand on which the said woman whose name she has heard is Ann Gregg asked this Informant for some a half penny worth of unbleached Thread That this Informant suspecting the said Ann Gregg had been Guilty of some Theft she this Informant seized hold of her & took from her two pieces of Red & White Linen Handkerchiefs sd which she had stolen out of the said Front Shop & were the property of Agnes Birbeck this Informant & more And at the same time this Informant saith the said Ann Gregg dropped from under her arm two pieces containing from three to six Handkerchiefs in a piece of eight Handkerchiefs which had also be stolen out of the sd Shop by the said Ann Gregg also the property of her the said Agnes Birbeck

Sworn before me the Day & Year afd _____
Thos Wilson

Mary Furnas

Deposition of Mary Furnas against Ann Gregg 1777

28

Chapter 3
1777 - Ann Gregg's First Offence.

Since Ann Gregg's first reported criminal offence was in her early twenties, I can't be sure it was her first actual offence. Perhaps she'd been offending, but just hadn't been caught, up to that point! Or maybe it was just that I couldn't find any records of her being through the courts; at least, not under the name of Gregg. The Cumberland Paquet was the earliest newspaper published covering Cumberland, Westmorland and Durham. Publication started in 1774, so it's quite possible that any earlier crimes by Ann were not reported.

Researching the life of Ann Gregg led to the discovery of a document dated the 15th of February, 1777. It was the court's examination of Mary Furnas, bookkeeper, of Wigton, taken on oath before Thomas Wilson. It read:

Cumberland Court

The information of Mary Furnas of Wigton in the said County, bookkeeper, taken on oath before me, Thomas Wilson, Doctor in Divinity, one of his Majesty's Justices of the Peace in and for the said County, this 15th day of February 1777.

The informant saith that yesterday in the evening about six o'clock she was sitting in her own back shop or apartment at Wigton aforesaid, when on hearing the tinkle of the bell at the front shop door she, this informant, immediately went into her said front shop and saw a woman standing with the door about half shut in her hand. On which the said woman, whose name she has heard is Ann Gregg, asked this informant for a halfpenny worth of unbleached thread. Then this informant, suspicious the said Ann Gregg had been guilty of some theft, she the informant seized hold of her and took from her two pieces of red and white linen Handkerchiefs which she had stolen out of the said front shop and were the property of Agnes Birbeck, the informant's niece. And at the same time, the informant saith the said Ann Gregg dropped from under her arm this purse containing from three to six Handkerchiefs in a piece of silk Handkerchief which had also be stolen out of the shop by the said Ann Gregg and was also the property of the said Agnes Birbeck.

Ann had been caught shoplifting, and it certainly looked like she was guilty. Her response to the accusation was, as you would imagine, to make an outright denial of the charge. In her examination, she spoke under oath before the same Thomas Wilson.

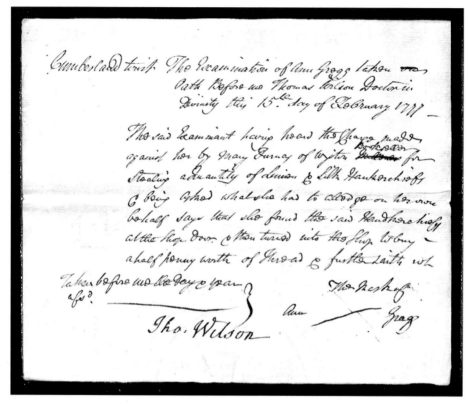

Ann Gregg's examination 1777

Cumberland Court

The examination of Ann Gregg taken on oath before me, Thomas Wilson, Doctor in Divinity this 15th day of February, 1777.

The said Examinant, having heard the Charge made against her by Mary Furnas of Wigton, Bookkeeper, for stealing a quantity of linen and silk handkerchiefs and being asked what she had to alledge on her own behalf, says that she found the said handkerchiefs at the shop door and then turned into the shop to buy a halfpenny worth of thread and further saith not.

Taken before me the day of the year aforesaid.

I like to think of her, declaiming her innocence as a naive fresh-faced young lady; but the fact is, that even if she were innocent, by virtue of her Traveller background, her reputation would have gone before her. Gypsies and Travellers had been persecuted across Europe for centuries. Newspapers and popular culture – literature, plays, pantomimes and paintings – had either depicted gypsies in overly romanticised terms or, more frequently, shown them as robbers, housebreakers and burglars, fraudsters and arsonists. If anything went missing, or a crime occurred, the gypsies were the first to be accused.

Again, this is not to say there's no truth in the accusations. But as a persecuted group, often spat at and derided, avoided and viewed with hatred and suspicion just for who they were – you can imagine that, for gypsies, the 'us' and 'them' divide grew wider, even in their own eyes. If you were so despised and demonised by the local community, what did you have to lose? Why should you respect English laws and ownership, if no-one respected you?

In Maslow's hierarchy of needs – food, water and shelter are the most basic requirements – and they are the main focus of people in extreme poverty. They rely on these basics for their life and their security, and until those things are secured and those fundamental needs are met, they can't give any importance to niceties like a sense of belonging, respect and esteem, or self-actualisation. Those at the very bottom of the social ladder often use desperate measures to survive – and often, those desperate measures become a way of life and who they have become.

So here was young Ann Gregg, around 21 years of age, caught red-handed, shoplifting linen handkerchiefs and pieces of silk, in the middle of Wigton.

Wigton is a market town twelve miles to the West of Carlisle, at the centre of the agriculturally rich Solway lowlands. The town's market and industry had been described at the time:

The principall traffick vended in this mercate is corn and yarne, for it is a great corne countrey all round this mercate, the soyl being naturally fertill. Great quantities of linnen yarn are likewise sold here by the neighbouring women, who make it their sole employment to spin all the year long (harvest time onely excepted). And there are a great number of linnen weavers in the adjacent villages, as well as in this town, who buy the same and work it into webbs, and have it bleached by their wives and fitted for Roseley & Carlisle fairs.

Weekly markets were held on Tuesdays, with two fairs annually, on St Thomas' Day and Good Friday.

There was also the fair at Rosley, to the east of the town, which was held on or about the 20th of February. This fair was said to be one of largest horse fairs and one of the largest gatherings of Travellers and Gypsies in northern England. I have no doubt that this was the reason Ann Gregg was in town, and it was probably why all the shopkeepers were on the alert, too.

Rosley Fair acted like a magnet to Travellers and Gypsies from many miles around. It had a long association with animal trading. Historically, it was on the main drovers' route – which, from the middle ages until the introduction of the railways, was the main route along which farmers would drive their stock from all over West Cumberland to Carlisle market. In the opposite direction, it was the route taken by black cattle (Angus) being driven south from Scotland. In the mid-18th century, more than 80,000 cattle passed through, annually.

The location also had a historical association with horses. The name "Rosley" is believed to be derived from the Scandinavian word "Hross", meaning horse, and the Old English word for a clearing, "Leah".

There is evidence that the origin of the fair lies with the Roman cavalry's existence there, 1,500 years earlier, when this area was one of the most heavily militarised in Roman England. A fearsome cavalry unit, the Ala Augusta Gallorum Petriana, was stationed at Olenacum, between Wigton and Rosley. They were there to defend the Roman Empire against the incursions of the Picts. Rome had lost the Ninth Legion, which would explain why Scotland had replaced Carthage as Rome's number one enemy and all-round "black beast". Roman mothers would frighten their children with the warning, "If you don't go to sleep, the Britanculi (little British devils) will get you." Some 1,000 horses were based there, which was twice the normal 500 – such was the scale of the threat perceived by the Roman command.

The enormity of servicing this military presence probably lies at the heart of the fair's beginnings. The cavalry would need a vast range of supporting trades, such as saddlers, bridle makers, farriers, and blacksmiths, as well as the ability to buy and sell horses. This naturally evolved into a livestock and horse fair, which continued to thrive and to grow, long after the Romans left.

Of course, wherever horses were traded, Gypsies followed. Despite being looked down on in their normal lives, when it came to trading horses, no-one knew the business better than the Travelling community. There were the usual stories about deceitful Travellers painting white horses black or using a multitude of tricks to make a horse look younger or more valuable. Most of these stories have some truth. On the opposite end of the spectrum, many farmers and carters enjoyed strong friendships with Gypsies, which were built on absolute trust and respect for their knowledge and skills in horse-breeding, handling and trading.

Ann Gregg would not have been in Wigton alone. When Travellers were on the move, they were always in groups of family or friends, and some travelled in troublesome gangs.

It's ironic that Rosley Fair's origins came from Rome's need to defend the area from Picts. Fifteen hundred years later, its market attracted Travellers, and the area now needed defending from the Greggs, who were descendants of the Picts.

Ann must have been arrested around the 5th of February, 1777, since she appears on the Carlisle gaoler Braithwaite Atkinson's epiphany petitions. The county gaoler sent a quarterly list of petitions to the quarter sessions, claiming from the County's coffers the expenses incurred by the gaol during that period. The epiphany petitions that year covered the period from 15th January to 9th April and they showed that Ann had been there for seven weeks.

Prisoners with no means of financial support could petition their parish of settlement for poor relief while they were held in gaol. If successful, the prisoner was given a weekly allowance of 9d (pence), which equates to £3.25 in today's money (2018). The petition shows that Ann was receiving this allowance.

Inmates were given a pint of gruel morning and evening, and 1lb of bread in the middle of the day. Gruel is a liquid of either water or a mixture of water and milk that had oatmeal boiled in it. Basically, the thinnest porridge imaginable, with very little substance. As basic as this diet seems, very few prisoners died in the prison: they at least had regular food, and a roof over their heads. This might not have been so bad for some of the dreadfully impoverished people who, by unfortunate circumstance, ended up there. Their allowance of 9d per week could be used to supplement their diets. Fresh vegetables were sold outside the prison walls by street traders and prisoners could also buy beer at a licensed tap room within the gaol. Water in towns in those times was usually contaminated and of very dubious quality, so most people preferred to drink beer. The water used for brewing ale came out of deep wells, and it had also been boiled in the pre-fermentation process, offering some protection against bacteria.

The prisoners' allowance wasn't just to be spent on food and drink; long-term felons had to provide their own clothing and footwear, as well as their own bedding. Prisoners could buy a "lapp of bedstraw" for a penny ha'penny. This had to be regularly replaced. Bedding was burned in the cells roughly once each month to fumigate the cell, killing the lice and fleas which spread gaol fever (typhus).

The Easter petitions of 1777 show that Ann was held over the full quarter, a period of 14 weeks. On the Midsummer records, she only appears to have been there for 3 weeks, which would take her incarceration up to approximately the 5th of August, 1777.

This could possibly have been because she was due to appear in court. A search through the local newspaper archives around this date resulted in the following report being found:

Cumberland Paquet 20th August 1777

At Carlisle assizes last week, Ann Gregg, for stealing wearing apparel, and John Graham for stealing several parcels of flax and lint, were severally found guilty.

A week later on August 19th, the same newspaper reported:

At the last assizes at Carlisle, Ann Gregg, for stealing two pieces of silk, received sentence of death...

I was astounded. Death, for a handful of squares of silk, a fraction of a second later, I took in the rest of the sentence:

... but was afterwards reprieved.

Being sentenced to death and being reprieved at the same session was not an unusual outcome, apparently.

Increasing fear of an ever-growing criminal underclass was causing great concern amongst the upper classes. The result of this was the introduction of the "Bloody Code", a term used to refer to the system of crimes and punishment at that time.

The Code was a list of the many crimes that were punishable by death. By the late 18th century, this included well over 200 separate capital offences. Guilty verdicts in cases of murder, arson, forgery, rape and treason unsurprisingly received capital punishment: the death sentence. However, there was also a list of lesser offences such as poaching, burglary, criminal damage, pickpocketing goods worth more than a shilling, and even being out at night with a blackened face (which might be termed as 'going equipped' for robbery, today) – which could all end in a trip to the gallows.

Ann's being sentenced to death for petty larceny would strongly suggest that this may not have been her first offence.

Also, the fact that her grandmother, aunt and uncle had been transported might also suggest that the Greggs were a family well-known to the judiciary.

An Account of Cash paid and laid out by Thomas Dixon
Gaoler for the County of Cumberland to the several persons
intitled to their Allowance Confined in the said Gaol since
the Tenth day of March 1770 to the 25th day of April following

To John _____ gay a Debtor 7. Weeks at 1s p. Week	0. 7. 0
To Sam. Bond Dr. 7. Weeks at 1s p.	0. 7. 0
To Robert Nook Dr. Do.	0. 7. 0
To Richard Raty Dr. 7. Weeks at 9d p.	0. 5. 3
To William Beanwin Dr. Do.	0. 5. 3
To Willm. Bigland Dr. 7. Weeks at 1s p.	0. 7. 0
To Thos. Dargue Dr. Do.	0. 7. 0
To John Dixon Dr. Dr.	0. 7. 0
To John Allison Dr. Do.	0. 7. 0
To John Gill Dr. Do.	0. 7. 0
To John Graham Dr. Do.	0. 7. 0
To James Gillbery Dr. Do.	0. 7. 0
To James Goodfellow 7. Weeks at 9d p.	0. 5. 3
To George Graham 3 Weeks at 9d p.	0. 2. 3
28. March Discharged	
To John Holloway 7 Weeks at 1s p.	0. 7. 0
To Joseph Hayton Dr. Do.	0. 7. 0
To Robert Latimer Dr.	0. 7. 0
To Thos. Stanger Dr. Do.	0. 7. 0
To Thos. Stephenson Dr. Do.	0. 7. 0
To John Sutton Dr. Do.	0. 7. 0
To George Wilson Dr. Do.	0. 7. 0
To John Purdy Dr. 3. Weeks	0. 3. 0
28 March Discharged	
Sargey Cash Dr. 2 Weeks at 9d p.	0. 1. 6
To Sargey Cash for her slander 3. Weeks at 9d p.	0. 2. 3
Discharged	
Thos. Robson a Debtor 7. Weeks at 9d p.	0. 5. 3
Thos. Slater 4. Weeks at 1s p. Discharged	0. 4. 0
Joseph Thompson 7. Weeks at 9d p.	0. 5. 3
Felony	
Jane Haugh 7 Weeks at 9d p.	0. 5. 3
Joseph McGaw Dr. Do.	0. 5. 3
John Pearson Dr. Do.	0. 5. 3
Willm. Wyburgh Dr. Do.	0. 5. 3
John Robson Dr. Do.	0. 5. 3
Ann Gregg 4. Weeks at 9d p.	0. 3. 0
William Briggs 2 Weeks at do.	0. 1. 6
William Cummins 1. Weeks	0. 0. 9
To 80 Wisps of Straw for the Gaol as p. test	9. 10. 9
	0. 10. 0
	£10. 0. 9

24th April 1770 _____ Court

I the abovenamed Thomas Dixon do upon _____ _____
oath Say That I have actually and bona fide paid the
several Sums abovementioned to the several persons
_____ _____

Carlisle gaoler Thomas Dixon's quarterly petition showing Ann Gregg as a Felon

36

Chapter 4
1778 - Carlisle Gaol.

The Easter petitions for Carlisle gaol show that Thomas Dixon was the new County gaoler. At that time, there were thirty-two prisoners incarcerated within the prison – Ann Gregg and seven other felons, as well as twenty-five debtors.

The other felons inside with Ann were Joseph McGee, John Pearson, William Wybergh, John Robson, William Briggs and William Currion. And the only other female felon was Jane Haugh, a Carlisle widow committed to the gaol on strong suspicion of being involved in stealing a number of fowls from the worshipful Dean of Carlisle, Thomas Wilson.

Normally, debtors and felons were kept apart in the gaol. Debtors who were incapable of paying off their debts, were imprisoned until they could find someone to pay off the debt, or until they could save up enough of their parish allowance to settle what they owed. However, many debtors could end up being financially worse off after a term inside, than they were before they entered prison. Having no money had brought them to prison in the first place – but having to pay for their keep in gaol pushed them further into debt. The small amount they could earn in prison barely covered their board and lodging. This changed after 1815, when all gaol keepers were paid from the rates, rather than from individuals.

Picking oakum was one of the tasks given to prisoners sentenced to hard labour. Debtors did not have to do any labour during their prison term. Many actually chose to pick oakum as a way of paying for their board, helping to keep their debt down, or even to pay it off, if they could.

"Junk", a term we still use today, was originally the name given to old ropes and cables that had once been used on ships. In prison, these were cut up, then finely picked apart into separate fibres to create oakum. The oakum was then sold and mixed with tar or grease to be used as caulking, to fill in the gaps between the wooden planks of ships to make them watertight.

Prisoners serving hard labour would cut the thick rope into two-foot lengths, then strike it with a heavy mallet, pounding it to remove the very hard tar in which it was coated. Once this was done, the lengths of rope were passed on to other prisoners – some of whom were serving a lesser sentence. They had to uncoil, unravel, unpick, and shred the rope into fibres.

The rope was held in place by an iron hook clamped between the prisoners'

Carlisle Gaol c1780

knees as they worked. The rope was still in its stiff, thick state of tightly bound threads coiled together, still coated in residual dried tar. The strands needed to be picked and unwound into corkscrew coils that were then rolled and rubbed on their knees until the fibres separated and could be pulled apart in shreds. Sometimes they would use an iron nail, a spike, a piece of tin, or a knife to work on the fibres, but being more dexterous, bare fingers were found to be the best tools. It wasn't an easy task. The work was monotonous, unpleasant, and it created sores on blackened fingers.

Carlisle gaol was located next to the southern gate into the city and was joined onto the citadel. It was first used as a gaol in 1611, after the previous county gaol had become so run-down that the majority of prisoners escaped. The city Court was in the citadel adjoining the gaol, making it all very convenient to hold prisoners prior to trial, and to try them; then, if found guilty, to incarcerate them – all without any transport being required.

Carlisle prison was built in a hexagon shape, with the governor's house in the centre and cell blocks radiating out from it. The governor's house was raised above the cells and the yard, so that he could look over them and see what was going on. There were separate cell blocks for debtors and those guilty of minor misdemeanours, and two blocks were reserved for women prisoners. Those sentenced to hard labour were also segregated in their own section. Next to

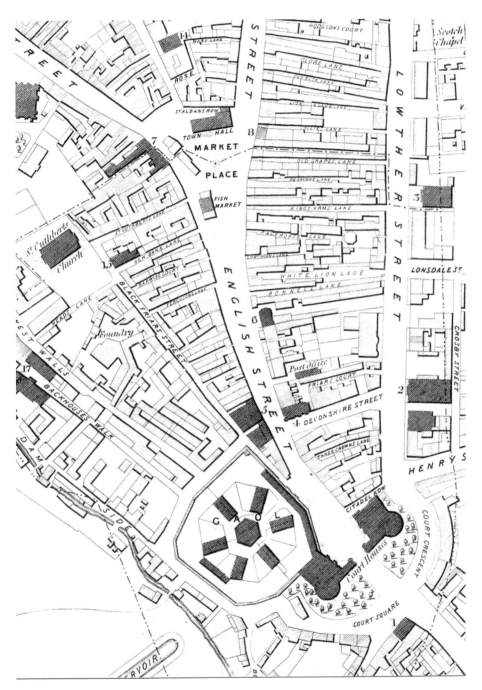

Street map showing Carlisle Gaol

the hard labour blocks was a row of treadmills, where prisoners had to walk the mill up to ten hours per day, pumping water into a storage tank. Hard labour prisoners were also employed in the stone yard, to break down large rocks into smaller stones that could be used for road building. Men and women sentenced to hard labour did the same work.

During the time that Ann was incarcerated, John Howard, a philanthropist and social reformer had become dedicated to public health improvements as well as prison reform. His father was a partner in a substantial upholstery business, and on his death, John inherited his father's considerable wealth.

In 1773, he was appointed high sheriff of Bedfordshire and supervision of its county jail became of one his responsibilities. He was shocked by the conditions he found there and visited other prisons in England, where the situation was no better.

Jailers were not salaried at that time, but lived off fees paid by prisoners for food, bedding and other facilities. This system meant that poorer prisoners lived in terrible conditions. Many jailers also demanded a payment before any prisoners were released, meaning that some people stayed in jail even if they were innocent or had served their sentences.

When John Howard raised his concerns about the prison system, this led to two 1774 parliamentary acts – one abolished jailers' fees; the other enforcing improvements in the system, leading to better prisoner health. Howard, however, felt that the acts were not strictly obeyed.

In 1775, he embarked on a tour of prisons in Europe, visiting Scotland, Ireland, France, Holland, Flanders, some German states and Switzerland, which resulted in the publication of his books, *The State of the Prisons in England and Wales* and *An Account of the Principal Lazarettos in Europe* (1779). A 'lazaretto' was a quarantine station for maritime travellers, to contain people with suspected disease and prevent epidemics being brought ashore from abroad. It had similar functions to a prison, but also appealed to Howard's interest in public health.

His research was groundbreaking and further raised awareness of the unhealthy and inhumane conditions of British prisons. The public outrage that Howard helped to generate later led to a national system of inspection, and the construction of new convict prisons for those serving long sentences.

Just the year after Ann was first incarcerated there, during his tour of prisons in 1778, John Howard visited Carlisle gaol, and his report gives a detailed insight of what it must have been like for Ann to live there.

CUMBERLAND

COUNTY GAOL at CARLISLE

| GAOLER | Braithwaite Atkinson, now Thomas Dixon. |
| | Salary £21 |

	Fees	Debtors}	
		Felons }	£ 0 : 11 : 0.
		Transports	£1 each to Whitehaven
	Licence	Beer. The tap let.	

| PRISONERS | Allowance | Debtors, on applying to the Justices some obtain a shilling a week, some nine pence. |
| | | Felons, nine pence a week before conviction, a shilling after. |

	Garnish	£0 : 1 : 0	
	Numbers	Debtors	Felons &c
	1774, Mar. 23	49	4
	1776, Jan 20	29	7
	1779, May 10	21	21
	French Prisoners	12 *	
	1782, Sep 1	30	9
	......., Sep 19	15	2

| CHAPLAIN | Rev, Mr. Farish | |
| | Duty | Sunday, Wednesday, Friday; first Sunday in the month, sermon. |

41

	Salary	£20 : 0 : 0
SURGEON	Mr Losh	
	Salary	£2 : 2 : 0 for attendance. Medicines paid for by bill.

The court spacious, 85 yards by 36: it was common to all prisoners; but now a part is appropriated to the felons, and separated by iron palisades. In the court is a chapel, built, as appears by the date, 1734. Five rooms for master's-side debtors: and as many on the common-side. For of these are 23 feet by 18 1/2. They have windows now opening into the court, as well as the street. Where there are so many rooms, not to separate the men and woman is certainly inexcusable.

The wards for felons are two rooms down a step or two; dark and dirty. One of them, the day-room, had a window to the street; through which spirituous liquors and tools for mischief might be easily conveyed: but is now bricked up. The night room over the felons' ward, which has been used as tap-rooms, seem to be intended for the women only, but in one of these, I also found three men and four women lodged together. In the court near the pump, there is the too common nuisance of a dunghill, which seems to have been accumulating for a year or two. Transports had not the King's allowance of 2s 6d a week. No infirmary: no bath.

Act for preserving the health of prisoners not hung up. Prison not white-washed for three years. Gaol delivery once a year. Few gaols have so many convenient rooms for common-side debtors. It is the more remarkable here, because there is no table signed by the magistrate to particularise the free wards. Some gaolers avail themselves of such a circumstance, and demand rent for rooms, which were undoubtably designed for common-side prisoners.

The gaol-fever, which some years ago carried off many of the prisoners, did not deter Mr. Farish from visiting the sick every day.

* PRISONERS OF WAR

CARLISLE, In the County gaol at Carlisle, in one large room in the debtors' ward, there were 12 French prisoners, May 10th, 1779. They were not supplied with hammocks as at Plymouth, Winchester &c. but lay on straw without coverlets. Their allowance, six-pence a day.

The summer of 1778 seemed fairly uneventful. Ann was still languishing in gaol. Then, two weeks before the end of the Michaelmas quarter, her sister Margaret appears on the list of prisoners in gaoler Thomas Dixon's petitions. This would have been around September 19th. Whether Margaret brought bad news to Ann, or if the timing was merely a coincidence, we cannot say; but eight weeks later, on 21st November, 1778, in the *Newcastle Chronicle*, and on the 24th of November in the *Cumberland Paquet*, it was reported:

Thursday se'nnight, one Ann Gregg, who received sentence of death at Carlisle assizes in 1777, and was afterwards ordered three years imprisonment, escaped the vigilance on Mr Dixon's turnkey, by assuming a different dress than that what she usually wore, and has not since been heard of.

So, Ann had escaped from prison in disguise! Had Margaret assisted Ann in her escape, somehow? Whose clothing was Ann wearing, that enabled her to walk out, unaccosted? Did she bribe a jailer? We can only speculate.

But it was very curious. Why did she feel the need to leave, right then? Ann had been in gaol since being arrested in February the previous year. Her sentence had been commuted to three years' imprisonment, so she was well into her prison term, half-way through, with not all that long to go. So, why abscond?

Then, the whole episode became even stranger, when the *Cumberland Paquet* reported, on the 1st of December, merely three weeks after her escape:

Cumberland Paquet 1st December 1778

Ann Gregg, mentioned in our last, has surrendered herself to Mr Dixon, the keeper of Carlisle gaol.

Ann had been on the run for only three weeks, then calmly went back to the gaol and handed herself in! This isn't easy to explain. Did she have some important business to do outside the prison? Did she find herself without a support network, during winter, and felt that she was better off in jail? Perhaps she thought her reprieve would be cancelled and she would have to face the death penalty again if she was ever caught. So, she came back to face the music. A doubtful and speculative explanation, but there doesn't seem to be any other.

Chapter 5
1779 - America, France and Ann.

Newcastle Courant, August 14th 1779

"At Carlisle Assizes this week, George Levingston and Thomas Williamson, for a burglary. Levingston received sentence of death. Williamson was admitted King's evidence, and acquitted, but to enter onboard a man of war. Joseph McGee, condemned last Assizes for a highway robbery, to be sent onboard a man of war. John Collingwood for horse stealing, Ann Gregg and twelve French prisoners to remain in gaol".

It had already been mentioned in John Howard's report on the Cumberland County gaol that there were twelve French prisoners imprisoned with Ann. The French prisoners were being held as prisoners of war because of their role in the conflict between England and America – the American Revolution, or War of Independence.

For more than a decade before the outbreak of the American Revolution in 1775, tensions had been building between American colonists and the British authorities. Attempts by the British government to raise revenue by taxing the colonies (notably, the Stamp Act of 1765, the Townshend Tariffs of 1767 and the Tea Act of 1773) met with heated protest among many colonists, who resented their lack of representation in parliament, and the demand for taxation. They wanted the same rights as other British subjects. Colonial resistance led to violence in 1770, when British soldiers opened fire on a mob of colonists, killing five men in what became known as the Boston Massacre. After December 1773, when a band of Bostonians dressed as Mohawk Indians boarded British ships and dumped 342 chests of tea into Boston Harbour, an outraged British Parliament passed a series of measures (known as the Intolerable, or Coercive, Acts) designed to reassert imperial authority. The eventual outcome of this was the Revolutionary War that began in 1775 and America's Declaration of Independence, in 1776.

America and England officially went to war on 19th April, 1775, this lasted until 1783. The French decided to back the U.S. in its military efforts until the U.S. had full independence from Great Britain. On February 6th, 1778, Benjamin

Franklin signed a Treaty of Amity and Commerce, as well as a Treaty of Alliance with France, making the fledgling United States and France allies against Great Britain in the Revolutionary War. After that, the treaty required France and the U.S. to work together on any peace agreement. French sailors who happened to be in British ports at this time were arrested and imprisoned to prevent them from joining the war. The twelve French prisoners in Carlisle gaol along with Ann would probably have been arrested at one or more of the Solway ports. They were held in Carlisle gaol in one room within the debtors' prison, while Ann was in the felons' block.

Quite by coincidence, Benjamin Franklin had another tenuous link with Carlisle gaol. Sailors had often talked about the calming effect that oil had when poured on "troubled" water. As a prolific scientist and inventor, Franklin had taken a personal interest in this phenomenon, which he called "wave stilling".

He wanted to examine how this worked, and in the 1770s, with fellow scientist, Sir John Pringle, he visited the home of William Brownrigg, a distinguished physician and Fellow of the Royal Society of London. The three went out on a boat on Derwent Water in Cumberland, where Franklin demonstrated the experiment.

Subsequently, a close friend of Brownrigg, the Reverend James Farish, Chaplain to Carlisle gaol, heard about the experiment, and wrote to Brownrigg: "I have since had the same accounts from others, but I suspect them all of a little exaggeration". Brownrigg forwarded the letter to Franklin, requesting that details of the experiment be sent to the Reverend. This correspondence was sent by Brownrigg to the Royal Society, where it was widely read and discussed. Had Reverend Farish not questioned this matter, it is doubtful that Franklin would ever have recorded the details of his experiment.

The midsummer petitions in 1779 show several new felons in gaol with Ann, including Elizabeth Cunningham. She had been arrested along with John Miller, James White and Christian Miller, for breaking into a shop. The Miller family were long-time associates of the Greggs, and a well-known Travelling family. Elizabeth Cunningham would later go on to marry Ann Gregg's brother, John.

At the midsummer assizes on August 17th, Elizabeth and Christian Miller (a female) were sentenced to be imprisoned for three months and were to be privately whipped.

Whipping had long been used as a method of physical punishment and humiliation. Public whipping entailed the person being stripped to the waist and tied onto the rear of a cart which was pulled along the street whilst the wrongdoer was being whipped, for all to see. This often took place in the street where the crime had been perpetrated. Private whipping was carried out inside the prison, with the felon tied to a whipping post. In both cases, the type of whip and the number of strokes was not determined at the time of conviction, but these details were left to the person who carried out the punishment. Carlisle gaol seemed to prefer the use of the birch for females, and birching was carried out "until their back be bloody.

During the midsummer quarter, another felon, Grace Wilson, and Christian White (perhaps the same person as Christian Miller) gave birth in the gaol, taking the total number of children in the gaol to five.

By Michaelmas, the adult population of the gaol had risen to nineteen debtors and twenty felons. Thomas Dixon, the gaoler, felt there was a significant threat of escape from having so many inmates, so he employed two watchmen to assist him. His petition for additional payment stated:

> To Stuart a watchman who assisted me in guarding the felons to prevent their escape being vey much thwarted for six weeks at 7s per week.

> £2 2s 0d

> To Mcintize another watchman four weeks for the same purpose at 7s per week.   £1 8s 0d

It must have been getting close to the epiphany assizes, since there was another entry: *To the price of a tub to wash the felons a little before the assizes.*
£0 4s 0d

Prisoners on the Thames

Chapter 6
1780 - The Thames.

By midsummer 1780, the two male prisoners who had been arrested with Elizabeth Cunningham and Christian Miller – John Miller and James White – were no longer appearing on the gaoler's petitions. They had both been sentenced to be "sent to the Thames" for three years.

Transportation to America had ceased, owing to the war. So, in 1776, the British government passed legislation to convert transportation sentences to hard labour on the Thames, for periods of three to ten years.

Duncan Campbell, the owner of the Tayloe, the ship that had transported Henry Gregg to America seven years earlier, was named "Overseer of Convicts" on the Thames and was awarded a contract to house convicts on ships and to use their labour. Campbell provided three ships: the Justitia, the Censor and a condemned East Indiaman, which he also named Justitia, unimaginatively enough. Collectively, these three ships could hold 510 convicts.

Prisoners were employed to work on the river – dredging it, maintaining its banks, and building new docks. The work was hard, the conditions were grim, disease was rife, and the mortality rate high. Inmates aboard the Justitia slept in groups in tiered bunks, with each person having a sleeping space of around 5ft 10in long and 18 inches wide. Not enough space to sleep in any other position than straight out. Rations consisted of ships' biscuits and pea soup, accompanied once a week by half an ox cheek, and twice a week by porridge and a lump of bread and cheese.

Many convicts would have preferred transportation to this floating hell.

Back in Carlisle, freedom at last was within reach for Ann Gregg. The midsummer quarter in 1780 was from April 1st to July 8th, a total of fourteen weeks. Ann is shown as receiving her allowance for eight weeks, so she must have been released on around May 13th, 1780.

Chapter 7
1782 - Making Smoke Screens.

Perhaps Ann had learned her lesson after spending three years in gaol, and came out a reformed woman, turning into a fine, upstanding citizen. No records nor newspaper reports of her committing any crimes, or being in prison, have come to light.

Or maybe she was still offending but just didn't get caught.

Researching Ann from 1782 onwards proved to be extremely difficult. Until a report appeared in the *Newcastle Courant* on 10th January.

Newcastle, January 10th 1782

THREE PERSONS *(Part of a Gang of Thieves) in PRISON here.*

A man who calls himself HENRY CUNNINGHAM, appears to be about 30 years of age, 5 feet 9 inches high, of dark swarthy complexion, thin faced, has black dull eyes, long black rough hair, a small scar of a slight wound under his left eye lately healed, a scar on his right jaw, and wants the first joints of the thumb and two first fingers on his right hand. (Remember his missing digits) *His present dress is an old coarse slouched hat, a black silk neckcloth, a coarse blue half wide coat, a fine light blue coat and waistcoat, and dirty buck or doe skin breeches. He says he was born in Wigton, in Cumberland, brought up a pitman, but for the last ten years has travelled the country, and sold earthen pots and mugs in summer, and coopered and mended lanthoras in winter. His principal residence hath of late been at Bishop Aukland, and at Barlow, near Winlaton, with some others of the gang.*

A little Woman who calls herself ANN HAMILTON, otherwise BROWN, says she has cohabited with said Cunningham as his wife for about five years past, but was never lawfully married to him, and was born at Dalkeith, in Scotland. She appears to be about 35 years of age, has light coloured hair, a fair complexion, a small round face, a slight squint with her right eye; her present dress is a black silk bonnet, a silk handkerchief about her head, a short red cloak, a remarkable beautiful flowered chintz gown, and a black quilted petticoat.

A Woman who calls herself MARY WILSON, says her maiden name was TATE, that she was born at Glasgow and is the wife of William Wilson, a Pitman, who lately entered into the marine service; she appears to be about 50 years of age, her stature is a degree under the middle size; she has brown hair, a scar on her forehead, another on her right cheek, another on her underlip on the right side; Her present dress is a black silk bonnet, a silk handkerchief about her head, a short scarlet cloak, a blue and white checked and spotted bed gown, a dark copper coloured camblet gown, and a black quilted petticoat.

The above described persons were apprehended in company together, and are part of a gang of thieves and pickpockets, who have for some time past infested the markets in this town, and generally resort to fairs in the country. Elizabeth Whitebread, the pickpocket, advertised in this paper the two last weeks, is one of the same gang.

Those who have any discovery to make, or anything to say concerning them, or who desire to see them, are to apply to the Town Clerk's Office.

A DISCOVERY of more of the same GANG.

THOMAS DOUGLAS and his wife, JOHN DOUGLAS his brother, and ELEANOR his wife, and DAVID their eldest son, aged about 15 years, and the noted THOMAS COLPITTS, otherwise STUART, and his wife, who have all lately resided or lodged, at or about the head of Gateshead, and on Gateshead Fell; other part of the gang reside at or near Bishop Aukland. They often change their names, and frequently rendezvous at the Crown and Cannon on Gateshead Fell, and have a Ware Room for the stolen goods, at or near the head of Gateshead, and another on the Fell.

Ann Hamilton was the first alias I found that was used by Ann Gregg. It would be easy to give an explanation why Ann was calling herself Hamilton when she was with this gang, but at this stage, it might spoil things for people like me, who like to be a sleuth and work things out for themselves.

One clue is the presence of Thomas Colpitts. He, along with the Douglases and Henry Cunningham, were tried in various places across the region throughout the early 1780s. Colpitts achieved local notoriety in the newspapers with arrests for stealing geese and sheep – from which he escaped. He was described as a Tinker, and with his wife, Ann Watson, he was convicted in the Newcastle Quarter Sessions. He was next heard of in Cumberland, where he was committed for stealing handkerchiefs.

Other reports on this gang call them "The Gang of Faws". Could this be the same gang mentioned thirty years earlier? The new generation? Who knows?

Gateshead Fell, or Sod-house Bank, as it was nicknamed, is south of Gateshead, on the way to Sunderland. At that time, it was one of the few remote and wild places left in north Durham. It was regarded as a no-man's land, an uncontrolled territory where crime took place and stolen goods were traded. It was described, thus:

The fell was studded with miserable mud cottages, inhabited by tinkers, cloggers and travelling potters, besom makers, egglers [itinerant egg sellers] and others of that worthy race called Faws. A good cottage is now a rarity even on Gateshead Fell.

This was the place where different gangs met, swopping and trading stolen goods. Other gangs travelled up there from York in the south, or came down from Berwick in the north. Built only two years earlier, in 1780, the Crown and Cannon Inn was the perfect meeting place and the landlady, "Gleed Bet" (squint-eyed Betty) welcomed the trade the gangs gave her. It was said that she never served a man she couldn't wrestle.

How do I know this is Ann Gregg? She started using aliases, and to say she was economical with the truth is an understatement. Over the following years, Ann also claimed to be married to at least three different men, and her given age varied wildly, too. Evidence shows that these tactics seemed to have been used by many petty criminals as a smoke screen. With no I.D. cards, no use of fingerprint analysis, no passports, no photographs, no DNA – this all meant that if someone simply lied about who they were, no-one would know. Ann travelled through Cumberland, Westmorland, Durham and Northumberland, so it would not have been difficult for her to reinvent herself wherever she was caught. The chance of her being transported or hanged was greatly reduced if there were no previous convictions. She could present herself as an innocent, each time.

Chapter 8
1783 - Violet Chambers.

Cumberland Paquet, 4th March 1783

Saturday se'ennight one Violet Chambers, (a notorious prostitute) in company with one Armstrong (a young fellow, as associate) both from Longtown, were committed to the county gaol in Carlisle, for the latter endeavouring to extort money from several people, under the presumption that Chambers was with child with them: This piece of villainy has been carried on with great success for some years by many abandoned wretches; but it is to be hoped the exemplary punishment those two culprits will meet with will put a total stop to this iniquitous practice in future.

Violet Chambers was from the same area as Ann Gregg. The above article says she is from Longtown, nine miles from Nichol Forest. She gave birth in 1775 to a son, a bastard child (the father is listed as George Harrington, a collector from Whitehaven) called George Chambers, who was baptised at Arthuret, which is six miles from Nichol Forest.

There is every chance that Ann and Violet knew each other. Ten years from then, and for several years afterwards, Ann and Violet's lives were intertwined, so I believed that her story was worth looking into.

Violet was a lady of the night, very well known in Carlisle and the English Border counties. Prostitution was rife at the time: again, abject poverty can probably be blamed. Soliciting was an offence, but it was rarely prosecuted, unless there was more to it than met the eye.

This extract from the Derby Mercury newspaper shows just how far news about Violet had travelled.

Derby Mercury 31st July 1783

We hear from Carlisle at the Sessions which began on Wednesday the 30th ult. that a Matter of Importance to the Public came before the Court there. One Violet Chambers, a common prostitute, together with

Parish Officers of Arthuret, were tried and indicted for a Conspiracy in obtaining Money at various Times from Mr. David Nelson, a very respectable Tradesman in Carlisle. The woman falsely pretending to be with child, and the Overseers under the Colour of and Pretence of doing the Duty of their Office, had so far intimidated Mr. Nelson, that although he was a total Stranger to the Woman, he suffered himself, for the Sake of his Reputation, and the Peace of himself and his Family, to be imposed upon by these Wretches; till finding their Importunities so frequently repeated, and not knowing when they might cease, he determined to prosecute them. They were all found Guilty, to the entire Satisfaction of a full Bench and crowded Court. The Woman received Sentence to stand in the Pillory three Times, and the Parish Officers were committed to Gaol, there to be imprisoned three Months, to give Security for their good behaviour for three Years, to pay a Fine, and stand committed till the Fine be paid, and security given.

So, true to Violet's form, judging by her previous conviction, she was still pulling the same stunt of faked pregnancy. Some poor stooge – an innocent soul – had been repeatedly press-ganged and blackmailed by Violet and two parish officials into paying up money, rather than suffer their bullying and the damage to his reputation.

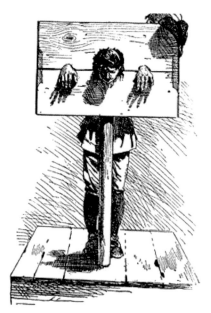

Violet was taking prostitution to a different level – and probably making more money from extortion than from the act itself.

The dates set for Violet to be pilloried were September 20th, 27th, and the final time was on October 4th.

The Pillory

Stocks and pillories date back for centuries. The stocks were mainly a mechanism used to confine the prisoner by their ankles and they usually held two people at once, seated. The pillory was a similar mechanism; however, it had three holes, one for the neck and smaller ones either side to secure the wrists. Again, these were often designed to take two prisoners at once. As late as the Georgian era, their use was still extremely evident, since on several days each week, there was some mention in the newspapers of them being used. Being pilloried was a real "naming and shaming" sentence. In Britain, the use of the pillory as a method of punishment was not abolished until 1837, despite several attempts to have it scrapped much earlier – in the 1780s; but the stocks remained for a few more decades.

Records show that the pillory under the market cross in Carlisle was repaired and painted prior to Violet's pillorying, suggesting that it hadn't been used for quite a while before that. The cost of the pillorying was £0 9s 6d, and Violet was provided with a supply of liquor throughout, which perhaps made it more tolerable.

The cost of Violet's pillory: £0 . 9s. 6d

She would have stood and rested her neck and wrists on the semi-circular cutaways of the lower wooden plank of the pillory, before the upper half came down in a scissor action. This locking device would hold her neck and wrists securely, so her head and hands were facing the jeering crowd before her. There was no escape: she was a captive target, vulnerable to whatever they could throw at her.

It was normal for the watching crowd to stand in front of the pillory to throw mud or rotten eggs; or they would sling the contents of buckets filled with blood and offal that had been brought from the butchers; or even dung and dead cats. The crowd were not allowed to throw things such as stones that could cause the victim physical harm. Pillorying could draw very large crowds, depending on the crimes of the person being pilloried. The crowds were often drunk and the pillorying could become rowdy, so extra constables were brought in. In Violet's case – 56 of them.

We hear from Carlisle that on Saturday last, Violet Chambers (a common prostitute) was put in the pillories there, agreeable to her sentence. The chief Constables, from different parts of the County, to the number of fifty six, attended to keep the peace. No disturbance happened; a few eggs were thrown at her, and, after standing an hour, she was taken down, and re-conducted to gaol, where she is to remain till the expiration of her sentence, and to be pilloried twice more.

Fifty-six chief constables sounds like a lot of strength for a common prostitute being pilloried for one hour! Violet had agreed to the sentence, so she wasn't going to make a great spectacle of herself. Maybe the constables were worried that more local businessmen like Mr David Nelson had been conned and might come out in force. Or perhaps there were rumours that Violet had been assisting the law in her own way, so they were expecting much more trouble. We'll never know.

The following January of 1784 we will discover that Violet rose to new heights. But first let's go back to the Greggs.

Chapter 9
1783 – Two Families Unite.

St Nicholas Parish Register showing the marriages of Ann Gregg to William Hutchinson, James Gregg to Jenny Hutchinson and John Gregg to Elizabeth Cunningham

Ann Gregg married William Hutchinson at St Nicholas Chapel of Ease, Nichol Forest, on 31st May, 1783. It was a double wedding: Ann's brother, James, married William's sister, Jenny, at the same ceremony. They were all married by the church curate, William Harrison, and both marriages were witnessed by the curate and Christopher Armstrong.

St Nicholas Chapel was built in 1756, and bears no resemblance to the present-day church, which was rebuilt in 1866.

In 1814, Archdeacon Walter Fletcher of Carlisle said:

"I visited this chapel on 31st August 1814 and found it a most miserable place, very small, with dirt floor and no alter. There was no chapel yard, some few had been buried in the field, without the service being read. Some were carried to Stapleton and the clerk there assured me that if the minister was not in, they just happed [wrapped] them up and left them."

I can imagine it wasn't the most romantic of churches, by today's standards.

At the time they were married, Ann was probably pregnant, since less than nine months later, she had her first child, Peter, who was born in the poorhouse in the neighbouring parish of Arthuret. According to the records, his father, William Hutchinson, gave his occupation as "tinker".

From 1783 until 1794, Ann gave birth to seven children. The last to be born was James.

On 16th September 1783, Ann's other brother, John Gregg, married Elizabeth Cunningham, also at St Nicholas Chapel, Nichol Forest. Elizabeth's father, Robert, was another well known member of the Gang of Faws.

Chapter 10

1784 - Smart Little Fellow.

Leeds Intelligencer, 20th January 1784

The week before last, a remarkably smart little fellow went to visit Yarm, and pretended to be Master of a ship laying then at Hull, for which he wanted to buy a large quantity of corn and timber; and actually agreed with a gentleman for rafts to the value of £600 for which he offered in immediate payment bills on one of the York banks for £1200 all of which he wished to have discounted. This the gentleman would have done had the money been at hand; for the bills seemed true and had been accepted; but soon, thinking it extraordinary a stranger should pay him so large a sum without receiving any value, he peremptorily refused. The little captain bore the disappointment with great good humour, and said, "He should go to Darlington and exchange 'em at the Bank there." In the evening he got into the company of a gentleman, who had retired from the sea service, and, after lamenting that his baggage was stopped by the storm, on the way from Hull, especially as he had put on his worst coat for the journey, he observed, "that they were both of the same size," and requested a suit of clothes for which he would pay, but payment was deferred till his return from Darlington, when he was to dine with him. He went there on a post-horse the next day, which without stopping at the Bank, he took on to Newcastle, and dismissed the boy who attended him, by saying the horses were paid for. He went forwards the same day to Hexham and attended the market, took samples of corn, smattered French, and seemed quite at ease, till on Thursday night he decamped. The Ostler pursued him for his reckoning, and did not overtake him till he had got into Carlisle, where on examination, The Little Dapper Captain was found to be a Female, and the very Lady who behaved so genteelly in this town about a month ago. Her name is Violet Chambers, a notorious courtesan, who had the honour to stand in the pillory at Carlisle in July last, for defrauding several tradesmen in that place of considerable sums of money, under a pretence of pregnancy. She is committed to gaol.

Violet Chambers was entering a whole new level of crime. Including impersonation and fraud! She cut such a convincing figure as a dapper little gentleman – and a sea captain, and even impressed with a smattering of French – that she managed to deceive a number of people on her way to ill-gotten gains.

Yarm's annual fair was probably the largest gathering of Travellers in the North East of England. It was a major three-day event, attracting farmers and traders from as far afield as Ireland. It was famous for being the biggest fair in the North East for cheese. Up to 5,000 head of Irish Cattle could change hands at the Fair. Despite horses being banned from the High Street until the third day of the meeting, hundreds were put through their paces for prospective buyers by the large Gypsy contingent who descended on the fair.

Just like all the other fairs where Gypsies traded horses, many apocryphal stories were passed down. One story describes how a handsome horse was being looked after by a young lad whilst his grandfather was in the pub. A prospective buyer approached the lad, who was holding the animal by the head, and he learned that the price of this fine creature was fifty pounds. The boy refused to allow the man to hold the horse's head himself, but he agreed to run the animal up and down the High Street. The buyer was mightily impressed by the horse's good form, and swiftly agreed to the price. It was only after the man had paid over the money and was leading the horse away that he discovered that the horse was blind. Needless to say, the lad had long since disappeared. As had his fifty pounds.

But back to Ann Gregg, or should I say Isabel Hamilton.

Chapter 11
1785 - Alias Hamilton.

On the 8th of March last, were committed to the Gaol at Durham, by the Reverend Dr Chaytor and Christopher Hill, Esquire, two of his Majesty's Justices of the Peace for the said county, two Men, who call themselves ROBERT CUNNINGHAM and GEORGE PATTERSON, charged with breaking into a Waggon at Darlington, in the said county, belonging to Mr John Bewick, and stealing thereout a Parcel of Goods, directed to Mr Scott, at Stockton.

The said Robert Cunningham and George Patterson are supposed to be part of a very numerous Gang of Thieves, who have, for some years past, infested divers parts of the county of Durham, and particularly Bishop Auckland, and it's environs.

The said Robert Cunningham appears to be between 40 and 50 years of age, is about five feet nine inches high, straight and tolerably well made, is rather of a fair complexion, with sandy short hair, turned up before, and wants his right thumb. Had on when apprehended, a brown coat, a green shag waistcoat, and fustian breeches.

The said George Patterson is son in law to Cunningham, appears to be about 24 or 25 years of age, about five feet seven inches high, is of a swarthy complexion. with regular features, long lank dark hair and wants the joint of his right thumb; had on when apprehended, a shabby drab coloured wide coat, a strait coat nearly of the same colour. with a blue waistcoat, and shabby coarse light coloured cloth breeches.

On Saturday last were also committed to the said Gaol, by Charles Spearman, Esquire, another Justice of the Peace for the said County, a Man who calls himself WILLIAM HAMILTON, and a Woman who says she is his Wife, and calls herself ISABEL, on suspicion of breaking into the Dwelling-house of one John Smith, of Stobba Lee, near Witton Gilbert, in this county, in the night of the 17th March inst. and cruelly beating the said John Smith and his wife, and stealing some money and goods thereout. The said William Hamilton and his wife are known to be related to and connected with the said Cunningham and Patterson. William Hamilton appears to be about 25 or 26 years of age, has a remarkable dark sullen countenance, with a strong black beard, and *loose long black hair, turned up before, and very bushy; is a middle sized man, and wants the thumb and the first joint of the fore and middle fingers of his right hand;* (Do you remember the missing digits) *had on, when committed, coarse light drab coloured cloaths. His wife appears to be upwards of 30 years of age, is of a swarthy dark complexion; had on when committed, a grey cloth capuchin cloak, which covered her nearly to the feet.*

Any one who can charge any of the aforesaid persons with any other offences, are desired to send Information thereof to the aforesaid Justices who committed them, or to the Clerk of the Peace for the said county.

You will notice that there are a lot of missing thumb joints and parts of fingers mentioned, for some reason. All the men mentioned in this report have missing digits, and in a previous report I quoted, a Henry Cunningham had a thumb and joints of two fingers missing – exactly the same as the person called William Hamilton, here... who is quite likely to have been William Hutchinson, Ann Gregg's husband. Confused? That was the whole point of the aliases.

As to the missing fingers, amputation wasn't legally used as a punishment for crime at this time, but you can't help wondering whether there was some kind of informal process going on – or a "code of honour" amongst thieves.

On the other hand, these men were likely to have worked with tools in their traditional gypsy and traveller occupations (as basket makers, potters and knife-grinders) and the regular cutting of wood and branches to make fires and bender tents would have had their own hazards, so maybe these missing fingers were accidental. It seems very odd and coincidental, though.

However, it is more likely that their missing thumbs arose from branding. This was used as a criminal punishment but was intended to identify convicts who pleaded "benefit of clergy". During this period, this plea was used to claim a lenient sentence in the case of first-time offences – and for people found guilty of manslaughter rather than murder. These criminals were branded on their thumb according to their crime: "M" for manslaughter/murder, "T" for thief, or "F" for felon. This identifier ensured that they received the benefit of clergy or leniency only once. At the end of the sessions, they were immediately branded in the courtroom, right in front of the audience.

Branding for those receiving benefit of clergy ended in 1779, although it continued for other criminals. In 1789, the final sentencing of branding was made at the Old Bailey.

In the case of these thumbless men, I suspect they either lost them through infection or more likely, deliberately cut them off at the first joint to conceal their 'label'. William/Henry appears to have got through three digits in total, up to this point.

Still... these amputations must have hampered their activities. Perhaps they left the sleight of hand crimes like pickpocketing and shoplifting to the women and others with a full complement of fingers.

But the big question this report provokes from me is: are William and Isabel Hamilton really William and Ann Hutchinson (nee Gregg)?

As time goes by, you'll see that Ann often uses the alias 'Hamilton' – a practice she seems to have started after her marriage. My guess is that she was trying to cause confusion between the names Hutchinson and Hamilton.

In fact, in 1785, there is a statement in the newspaper that makes the direct link between Ann Gregg and Ann Hamilton, identifying her as one and the same.

Cumberland Paquet 19th April 1785

Whereas a warrant was granted by Thomas Denton Esq. one of his Majesty's Justices of the peace, for the County of Cumberland, on the 7th day of April 1785, upon an information made before him for that purpose, by Joseph Martindale of Hesket new Market, in the said County, Dealer and Chapman, to search the dwelling house of one John Neve, of Hafell Head, near Wigton, in the said County; that upon such search, the following goods were found, which there is reason to believe have been feloniously stolen. Part of which Goods, one Ann Gregg, otherwise Hamilton, claimed to be her property. The said Ann Gregg, otherwise Hamilton, and one Margaret Neve otherwise Hamilton, were thereupon brought before the Magistrate, as persons suspected of having stolen the said goods, and committed to Carlisle Gaol, until further examination.

If therefore any Person or Persons having lost such goods as are hereunder described will immediately apply at the Clerk of the Peace's office, for the County of Cumberland, the said goods will be produced to them for their inspection.

61

This is the first evidence of Ann using Hamilton as an alias. Although Ann was committed to gaol "until further examination," there can't have been enough evidence to indict her. There are no records of her being in gaol.

So, she either fronted out her thieving, declaiming her innocence – and nobody claimed the property as their own (through either ignorance or intimidation). Or she gave a feasible excuse for them being in her possession, and there was no proof of her stealing them herself. Case dismissed. Released without charge.

On November 30th, 1785, Ann had her second child, a daughter. Elizabeth was baptised at Nichol Forest, but it wasn't long before Ann was active again.

Less than a month afterwards, she's in the news once more; this time, in Whitehaven.

Cumberland Paquet 21st December 1785

A Train of circumstances, relative to shop-liftings and thefts of various kinds, has appeared during the examination of Ann Gregg (one of the women committed last week from hence to Carlisle gaol) the catalogue of which would fill half a newspaper. Numbers of shopkeepers in this town (Whitehaven) have suffered a little; and the gang to which she and Mary Fox (her present fellow prisoner) belong, do business in no less than four counties. A correspondence between the different members of this numerous and dangerous fraternity, has been carried on by a more regular method than the honest part of the world can imagine; and the dissolving of such an infamous league would be an achievement highly beneficial to society. Some enquiries are on foot, which will probably contribute largely to this end; but experience proves that the exertions of individuals are seldom vigorous enough in the encountering such great objects; - the vigilance of the magistracy ought to be followed by the determination of those concerned to bring to justice such offenders as are taken; and this is perhaps not to be fully effected without associating for the general welfare. - This, after all, would probably strike a greater terror in the minds of the dissolute and abandoned, than any other means whatever.

Ann was making major news, as a leading character in a nationwide network of organised crime. A kind of gypsy mafia. She was becoming something of a folk legend. According to the report. she and her gang were apparently rampaging around four counties, striking fear into the eyes of shopkeepers and anyone with a handkerchief. The media called for the strongest justice possible to protect the people from this menace.

This story even made the newspapers in places as far away as Bath, in the West Country. – and her gang was apparently creating something of a national emergency.

Bath Chronicle 29th December 1785

Gangs of thieves, cheats, and robbers have dispersed themselves over the whole Kingdom, and have entered into combinations, and regular correspondences, with a degree of rhythm and regularity, which would create astonishment to those unacquainted with their arts. Two women of the Northern gang were apprehended here (Whitehaven) a few days ago, and in the course of their examination discovered a catalogue of thefts and shop-liftings to fill half a newspaper. They are called Ann Gregg and Mary Fox and have for some time carried on their business in four counties. The people of Carlisle have been under the necessity of entering into association for mutual defence against these plunderers, and most other towns and villages are following the example. In short, those who have any property have no other means of securing it, than by giving each other mutual support.

It's not surprising that Ann had found her way to Whitehaven. There would be rich pickings, there. In 1785, it was the most inhabited town in Cumberland, with a population exceeding 10,000. It was the 6th largest seaport in England.

Seven years earlier, in 1778, during the American War of Independence, the town had been attacked by the U.S. naval commander, John Paul Jones.

An unattributed article on the Whitehaven and Western Lakeland website describes the attack:

Late at night on April 22nd 1778, the USS Ranger stood about 2 miles off the unsuspecting town of Whitehaven on a clear but cold and frosty night. Two boats were let down into the water and filled with about 30 men armed with pistols and cutlasses. John Paul Jones took charge of one with his Swedish second in command, one of the few he felt he could trust, Lieutenant Meijer. The other boat was commanded by Lieutenant Wallingford of the US marines and Midshipman Ben Hill. The two boats

63

rowed against the tide for 3 hours to reach the harbour, where Jones planned to destroy hundreds of ships by setting them alight as they lay stranded in the low water and packed tight together, several abreast, against the piers.

The intention was for Wallingford's men to burn the ships in the northern half of the harbour as Jones led a raid on the fort to spike the guns. This was vital to secure escape after their mission, as the guns of the fort covered the harbour entrance and could have blasted the small boats as they made their retreat. John Paul Jones landed first, near the battlements. As it was a cold night, the guards had gone into the guardhouse at the back of the fort to keep warm. According to Jones, he himself led the surprise attack. By climbing on each other's shoulders, they managed to silently scale the walls, enter the fort, burst into the guardhouse and secure the surprised guards without bloodshed.

He left Lieutenant Meijer guarding his boat, which was wise, as according to the Swede, the rest had concocted a plan to take the boat and leave Jones behind, had he not been successful. In fact, it was not until John Paul Jones himself stood on the battlements, gave his men reassurance and encouraged them to become heroes, that they plucked up courage to join his mission.

Having secured the fort, Jones took Midshipman Joe Green to spike the guns at the Half-moon Battery which lay on the shore, 250m from the fort, behind Tom Hurd's rock. This probably contained 32-pounders that could fire over a mile and it was thus vital to the escape that these were incapacitated. He sent the rest of his men to burn the shipping in the southern part of the harbour.

Whilst their Captain was disabling the guns, Wallingford and his men landed at the Old Quay slip and headed straight to the pub and got drunk. That might be a little unfair, as it is thought Nicholas Allison's public house was on the Old Quay near the ships, so they actually secured the house to make sure no-one left and gave the game away. They also later told Jones that they needed to get a light for their incendiaries, but apparently, they did make very free with the liquors.

Whitehaven survived the American invasion relatively unscathed, because the planned fires were contained to just one ship and didn't spread to others in the local fleet. Although John Paul Jones's invasion failed, it did make a lasting impression:

Britain changed its security strategies to better protect it from coastal invasion in the future.

In Ann's time, the port of Whitehaven was booming; with ships arriving from all over the world, carrying a diverse range of cargoes such as sugar, timber, tobacco, rum and slaves. Whitehaven was also the gateway for people from Scotland and Northern England to emigrate to a new life in the Americas.

Ann was certainly becoming a notorious criminal, with nationwide newspapers thoroughly vilifying her. I wondered what the general public must have thought about her. At this time in history, many people viewed criminals and law-breaking as heroic and courageous, and the activities of robbers and villains were often widely celebrated in popular culture. Stories of daring criminality were widely reported in lavish, dramatic detail in printed pamphlets, books and newspapers, or featured in plays and song, and they generated high levels of public interest in every corner of the country. Partly, in a world with little leisure and entertainment available, the melodramatic and sometimes bloodthirsty descriptions in the press served the same purpose as horror and drama on film and TV today. Although a great many of the population were illiterate, so much of the news travelled by word of mouth. Quite possibly, some people saw criminals as committing political acts of heroism or social justice: the poor fighting back against the rich. But whether she was a hero or villain, Ann was certainly starting to fit the bill, providing fodder for the masses, with her latest appearance in court being reported nationally. And things were changing. Rising poverty and crime levels were affecting even the poor, so perhaps Ann was despised, rather than admired. Certainly, her being a gypsy gave her a bad reputation from the outset. They were the real underclass of society – demonised by most.

Although the report of 21st December, 1785, said that Ann had gone to Carlisle gaol, I can't find anything to tell me how long her sentence was. The next time she appears is the following month, in a humorously ironic news report, with a reference to "all her honourable appendages" to her name.

Cumberland Paquet 25th January 1786

Mrs Greggs, with all her honourable appendages to that name, has made a very short visit to her old residence; indeed it was contrary to her inclination that she went, as by that trip, she was prevented from pursuing a very profitable business. However, as it will be for the interest of society that she should keep house for a certain time, it is hoped particular notice will be taken of her description in the Hue & Cry.

I liked that: "a very short visit to her old residence" – a poetic way of saying she'd been back in gaol again, on a short sentence. And although her "trip" was against her wishes, it really was an even shorter stay than expected, as I learned after reading the next newspaper instalment of her dramatic escapades.

Cumberland Paquet 1st February 1786

Broke out of Carlisle gaol in the said County on Thursday morning the 12th of January last

ANN HAMILTON, alias GREGG, alias CARRICK, about 30 years old, five feet six inches high, red hair, long visaged [long face], of a ruddy complexion; her usual dress was a light cotton gown, dark cotton bed gown, and red cloak.

The said ANN GREGG alias &c. was committed to the said gaol on 11th December last, for feloniously stealing, taking and carrying away Seven Cards of Lace, and Three Pieces of Ribbons, of the value of five pounds, the property of Hannah Shaw, of Egremont in the said County, Milliner.

She is well known in this County, having been frequently described in the "Hue & Cry" of this paper, and particularly in that of the 13th September last.

ALSO broke out of the House of Correction in Cockermouth, on the 19th, 20th of February Instant, Elizabeth GREGG, alias THOMPSON, about Twenty eight Years old, and Five feet Three inches high, or thereabouts; Black hair, long visaged, pale Complexion, thin nose.

ALSO Broke out of the said House of Correction, at the same time, ANN WILSON, alias MILLAR, alias GREGG, about Twenty Years old, and Five Feet One Inch high, or thereabouts, brown hair and curled much, round visaged, pale complexion.

The two last named persons are Convicts and sentenced at Christmas sessions 1785 to be transported for seven years; and are known in this County, as well as the said Ann Hamilton.

Whoever apprehends the above named three persons, or any one of them, shall be handsomely rewarded by the respective Keepers of the said Prisons.

Once more, the gang's housebreaking skills had usefully worked in reverse, and the three women had broken out of prison, somehow. Again.

Ann continues to cause confusion with her aliases. In this case, there are two Anns who have both used the name "Gregg" in the past. Fortunately, this article explains itself. Our Ann is the first Ann, alias Hamilton, alias Carrick. The age is more fitting, for one thing, as is the use of the name "Hamilton" again. There is also a good clue to follow in the text, giving the date of a previous edition of the paper: 13th September 1785, which has more information.

Cumberland Paquet 13th September 1785

HUE & CRY

COUNTY OF CUMBERLAND

STOLEN GOODS

WHEREAS THOMAS COLPITTS, otherwise JOHNSON, was committed to the House of Correction at Cockermouth on the 3rd instant by J. C. SATTERTHWAITE, Esq. one of his Majesties Justice of the Peace, in and for the said County, charged with having feloniously stolen a Parcel of Silk Handkerchiefs, and one pair of black worsted stockings, the property of Mary Crossthwaite of Keswick, in the said County, Shopkeeper; the said COLPITTS was traced into a field near Keswick, where the goods were found tied up in a Piece of Linen Check, and hid under a Hedge. The following articles were found tied up in the same bundle, viz. One Silver Table Spoon, Mark F.L. in a cypher. Four new Silver Tea Spoons, not marked; Two Pieces of Thread Lace Edging, upon Cards; the Shopkeepers Mark upon the Cards, cut off; a small piece of new Blond Lace, a pair of Iron Pincers, and an Iron Pick Lock.

The said COLPITTS, on his Examination, called himself JOHNSON; but hath since acknowledges his real name to be COLPITTS; says he was born near North Allerton, in Yorkshire, brought up a shoemaker, but has not followed that branch for some years past; acknowledged himself a deserter from his Majesties 9th Regiment of Foot, having enlisted with a party of that Regiment at Durham, and soon afterwards deserted from York.

Colpitts is well made, five feet eight inches high, about Forty Years of Age, rather grey headed, Hazel Eyes, Large Roman Nose, which with his forehead is full of pimples; had on when apprehended, an old dark grey coat with white metal buttons, a blue grey coat with black buttons, a

67

kind of brown ribbed fusileers waistcoat and breeches; is said to have been tried and punished with whipping at Durham about a year ago.

The said Colpitts was accompanied by a woman who calls herself ANN HAMBLETON of Moss Side in Nichol Forest, who is suspected to be an assistant to him in committing the aforesaid felony, and suspected to have been guilty of many other robberies in this County, from the various articles found in a large bundle, which she left in the care of Mrs How, Innkeeper, in Keswick, on the day when the felony was committed, but on being apprehended, denied the said bundle and articles therein contained to be her property. The said Ann Hambleton is about forty years of age, tall, and stout made, marked with small pox, and has for some years trailed up and down the Country selling Earthenware, and made her escape from the Constable as he was carrying her before a Magistrate to be examined.

The said bundle contained the following articles, viz. a piece of Irish Linen, cut at both ends. Ten Black Silk Barcelona Handkerchiefs; four Checked Silk do.[ditto] One Sucee, and one chocolate do. Six printed cotton handkerchiefs; One printed do. of a red ground. Five printed handkerchiefs, chocolate colour ground. One piece of Satin gauze striped ribbon (the mark tore off the Wood Rolle) the ribbon is wrapped up in an old letter directed to a Mr. Mounse, in Whitehaven; two bails of mixed worsted; a pair of grey yarn hose; together with some trifling articles of woman's apparel.

The above goods are lodged in the hands of the Constable of Papcastle, where any person whose property they are, may make their claim.

Comparing this report to the article in the Cumberland Paquet dated February 1st, this suggests that the woman in this article is Ann Gregg. It certainly sounds like her style, stealing fabrics etc. Her age doesn't seem to fit, but who's to say there isn't more blatant lying going on? She was a chameleon. And Hambleton and Hamilton sound the same. The real give-away is that Ann says she is from Moss Side, Nichol Forest, which is the home of the Greggs. If only the Justice of the Peace in 1785 had computers, like we do, now! A quick check of the parish registers for Nichol Forest and its surrounds very quickly shows that there was no Ann Hambleton – nor any other Hambleton – baptised, married or buried in the area. That's a pretty good clue that it was Ann Gregg – as was the fact that Ann's father was Shadrach Gregg, an earthenware hawker (which she claims to be her trade).

And she is with Thomas Colpitts, one of the old gang.

So, there she is, asking Mrs How, the innkeeper: "Look after my bundle." And soon after, "That's not my bundle! Never seen it before in my life!"

Who would you believe?

1785 - 1786 was a proving to be a busy time for Ann. The next we hear of any of her gang, is in Newcastle.

Chapter 12
1786 - Newcastle

Newcastle Courant 21st June 1786

A SHOP-LIFTER committed to Gaol Here.

A woman who calls herself Elizabeth Smith, (wife of Thomas Smith, late of Durham, Hatter) but whose real name is Gregs or Gregson and belongs to Cumberland, on Saturday last was detected stealing goods in a Linen Drapers shop in this town (Newcastle) and was committed to gaol last Monday, to take her trial at our next assizes; she appears to be about thirty years of age (and says she is older) of brown complexion, rather strong made and something above the middle stature; she wears at present a black silk bonnet, a black silk hood, which draws with a string quite round her face, a long grey duffle cloak, bound with blue ribbon, and its hood is lined with blue Persian silk, a printed cotton gown with a buff cloud, a red Stormont stripe and black and blue sprigs; a blue petticoat and a blue and white checked apron.

There were found upon her (besides the goods she was catched stealing) two black silk Barcelona handkerchiefs, in one piece a yard and a half of purple figured ribbon, and a yard and a half of white figured ribbon, a silver teaspoon, a twenty shilling note of the British Linen Company, at Edinburgh; three guineas of gold, and a quantity of silver, among which were several crowns and half crowns.

It is said she lately broke out of Carlisle gaol, and belongs to a gang of Shop-lifters and Pick-pockets, who frequently rendezvous at Gateshead Fell, Barlow and Bishop Aukland, and are connected with other gangs of thieves on the Borders of Northumberland, and Cumberland.

She says one Jane Walker, wife of John Walker, late of Durham, hawker and pedlar, is one of her accomplices. She lodged with a woman in Gateshead, who is said to be a harbourer of thieves, and is commonly called Gleed Bet [Betty with a squint].

All persons who have discovery to make, or any accusation to bring against the said Elizabeth Smith, otherwise Gregs or Gregson, or those who desire to see her, are to write to the Town Clerk, or apply at his office."

What an amazing description. It's very difficult to read that, and not picture her. This appears to be our Ann Gregg, although an Elizabeth Gregg also escaped from prison at the same time as she did. They all swapped identities and names so frequently, it's hard to say who is who, on the surface. And equally, the newspapers can only report the facts as they know them. However, a later news report clarifies the issue and confirms that this is yet another alias Ann Gregg used. And in fact, the identity of this woman was later revealed to be Ann Gregg.

Ann might have been born more than 250 years ago, but I feel that I know her. It really isn't difficult to feel an emotional attachment, and some empathy with her. She may seem to be a lying, thieving, deceitful, common criminal, but poverty and hardship had led her down a path with no return. If society paints you as a rogue and thief from birth, you might as well be one. Generations of racism and poverty made her this way. And for all her "badness" I can't help but feel a growing fondness for her and her, fearless, devil-may-care ways.

This isn't a work of fiction: she was a real person, and she was becoming more alive as her story unfolded.

How long could Ann keep this up? She seemed to be in prison more often than she was out! I had so many questions. Why didn't she get a harsher sentence, this time? She had been sentenced to death only nine years earlier for stealing two silk handkerchiefs, yet here she was, stealing much more and only getting a few months in prison! Why wasn't she transported? I've read about so many others being transported for much less. She'd broken out of prison twice (so far) and nothing seemed to have been done about it.

What about her husband, William? Ann seemed to find time to get pregnant and have children in between her bouts of crime. I noted down in my timeline the baptism records of her children and calculated approximately when they must have been conceived – and everything fits the timescale.

There definitely seems to be something enigmatic about Ann, to be getting away so lightly. Or could she have just been taking advantage of the situation, given the peculiarities of the justice system of the late 1700s?

Through further reading, I'd learned that the vast majority of criminal cases during the late 1700s were brought before local magistrates, who dealt with crimes without the benefit of a jury. Magistrates were unpaid officials drawn from the ranks of the wealthy, and as amateurs, they were expected to defend the English law. As a result, many magistrates were easily corrupted. It was commonly thought that the greatest criminals were officers of justice. Although magistrates were extremely powerful men, many found their duties extremely burdensome and often dealt with their heavy caseloads with great reluctance.

So, it would have been quicker and more lucrative to take a bribe, not bother about the detail, and give a short sentence.

Another point for consideration is that, at the end of the eighteenth century, women serving short terms of imprisonment or awaiting trial would have been confined in local houses of correction, or country gaols. Many of these had large shared cells, which allowed free association between female and male prisoners. These institutions were notorious for corruption and abuse, with many reports suggesting that women confined in gaols like this were vulnerable to sexual exploitation and susceptible to offering sexual favours in return for rewards.

Somehow, Ann must have used money, connections, deception or charm to work the system and evade harsher sentences. But this time, it seemed that her past was catching up with her. Ann had been arrested on June 21st, and her case came before the courts on August 19th, 1786.

Newcastle Courant 19th August 1786

At the Assizes held in and for this town and county, before Francis Buller, Esq; one of the Justices of his Majesty's Court of King's Bench, and John Heath, Esq; one of the Justices of his Majesty's Court of Common Pleas, which ended on Wednesday last, the nine following felons were tried and convicted, the three first capitally, and of consequence received sentence of death, viz. John Thompson, Mariner, for stealing a silver watch privately from the person of Jonathan Simpson, Ship-Master; this was done on shipboard on the river Tyne: and Thompson was indicted for another felony, committed in a ship on the river; but being convicted of the first mentioned crime, he was not tried for the other. Henry Jennings, Labourer, for stealing a bay gelding, the property of William Donald. Jennings was also indicted for two other felonies; but being convicted of the horse stealing, he was not tried for the others. William Bell, Labourer, for stealing in the Dwelling-house of Thomas Ogilvie, money to the amount of £6 8s. 6d. This convict is only about 15 or 16 years of age, and is reprieved: the two former are left for execution.- Robert Thompson was indicted for two burglaries and larcenies; but being acquitted of the capital part of those crimes, he was convicted only of grand larceny within the benefit of the statute, and was sentenced to be transported beyond the seas for the term of seven years.- Elizabeth, wife of Thomas Smith; Elizabeth, wife of William Thompson; Mary, wife of John Brown; and Frances, wife of James Atkinson; severally for grand larceny within the benefit of the statute, were sentenced to be privately whipped, and afterwards committed to the house of correction; there to be kept to hard labour for the term of one year.- Jane, wife of Walter Clark, for grand larceny within the benefit of the statute, sentenced to be privately whipped, and afterwards committed to the house of correction; there to be kept to hard labour for the term of two years.- These five female convicts are part of a certain notorious gang of thieves, many of whom are now pretty well known among the people of trade in this town, particularly the Linen-drapers; and such discoveries have lately been made, as we hope cannot fail of soon extirpating the whole gang. The above woman, who calls herself Elizabeth, the wife of Thomas Smith, her real name is said to be Ann Gregg, shortly before she committed the crime here, for which she is now under punishment, was in Carlisle gaol charged with a felony, but broke out and escaped before she got her trial.- The above Frances Atkinson has a boy only about six years old, which she takes with her into shops, and has taught him to be very dextrous with taking up and going off with goods, whilst she is engaging the attention of the shopkeeper another way.

So, things were starting to catch up on Ann. One year's hard labour and a private whipping! Perhaps the punishments were starting to fit her crimes! She was still very lucky to only receive this punishment. For grand larceny (let alone for those accumulative repeat crimes and jailbreaks), she could easily have been hanged – which, in those days, was not done quickly.

She would have been drawn in a cart through the streets, then given the opportunity to address the crowds and confess her sins. She would then have stood on the back of the cart under a gibbet, with the noose around her neck, and the cart would have been driven away. This resulted in slow strangulation.

If hanging was not the sentence given, Ann could very easily have been transported for a minimum of seven years – which usually meant for life. Very few convicts ever returned to England after the completion of their sentence, due to the cost of travelling home.

As barbaric as a private whipping sounds, Ann must have felt that she got off lightly. The number of lashes was normally left to the person carrying out the punishment and was often based on the fitness of the prisoner, she might have fared badly. From the previous description of Ann, she sounds fairly strong and fit, so she would probably have suffered the worst sort of lashing. Unless she managed to bribe her way out of it.

Chapter 13
1787 - Arrested as a Vagrant

Ann survived her punishment and was released after serving her prison term of one year in June/July, 1787.

Working backwards from the baptism of her next child, William, I calculated that she hadn't waited long after her release to get pregnant again.

The next find was only a few months after her release.

Newcastle Courant 22nd December 1787

There is little doubt that the vagrant apprehended at Appleby is the celebrated Ann Gregg, alias Garrick, alias Hutchinson, alias Smith, alias Orton, who (amongst other wonderful escapes) made her escape from the gaol at Carlisle on 12th January, 1786, not choosing to be tried for stealing sundry millinery articles in different shops at Egremont.

That was surprisingly silly, for Ann. From the reference to "the celebrated Ann Gregg" and the national news coverage, I get the feeling that, by then, Ann's reputation preceded her, and wherever she went, she was known. So, to be picked up as a vagrant – with a profile as widely known as hers – was just asking for trouble.

Anti-vagrancy measures were in operation to prevent "idleness" and used particularly against poor people deemed to be "wandering and begging".

Legislation like the Poor Law did provide support, initially through the parish, and by this time, through the county – for the "deserving poor" who could not work because they were sick, disabled, or old. Only in their own place of settlement, however, because nowhere else wanted to pay for their upkeep. However, legislation also punished those who "would not" work and was used to keep the poor in their place – literally. Anyone poor without a "pass" entitling them to live in the area could be whipped, imprisoned, or be rounded up by constables and delivered by "vagrant contractors" to their old place of settlement.

Appleby was on the main route from Cumberland to Durham, and roughly half-way, so a good resting place for people and horses. It was a well-known fact that vagrants used this route, and Appleby had way above the average number of constables looking to catch them. But it was no use crying: Ann had been nobbled again and would be held in Appleby gaol, waiting for her vagrancy examination.

Newcastle Courant 29th December 1787

VAGRANT in APPLEBY GAOL

Committed to Appleby gaol, by William Stephenson, Preston Esq; one of his Majesties Justices of the Peace for the County of Westmorland.

ANN ORTON, a Vagrant, aged about 28 years, who, in her examination, taken before the said Magistrate, saith she was born in the Parish of Moresby, in the County of Cumberland, and that about four years ago she was married to one William Orton, of Leeds, in the county of York, Hawker and Pedlar.

When apprehended she had several articles of Drapery Goods in her possession; supposed to be stolen, and it is presumed she is the person who hath been confined in different prisons in the north of England, by the names of Gregg, Hamilton and Smith, for various crimes.

Whoever can give information of any offence committed by the said Vagrant, so as she may be prosecuted, is desired to transmit an account thereof previous to the next General Quarter sessions of the peace to be holden in and for the County of Westmorland.

Appleby Dec 12th 1787

At first glance, this report seemed to open a can of worms. Ann now declares that she's married to William Orton. I have to confess that my heart did sink when I read this, thinking that all my research was wrong.

But she says she was born at Moresby, as was Ann Gregg. She had been stealing drapery goods, which Ann liked to steal. And if she said she got married four years before, that would have been 1783, the same year Ann married William Hutchinson. Too many coincidences. So, this begs the question: is William Hutchinson using the alias William Orton?

I can find no evidence of a Gregg/Orton marriage at Leeds. My opinion is that this is just another of Ann's elaborate guises, and William Orton is her husband, William Hutchinson.

Ann was either very lucky, or very well-connected, managing to intimidate the possible witnesses, or not guilty, as the next month's news read:

Cumberland Paquet January 13th 1788

How greatly the character of Mrs Gregg, alias &c. &c. &c. Must have been traduced! - Before her arrival at Appleby gaol, a thousand tongues were wagging against her; now, when a general challenge has been given, all her accusers are mute, and the woman, mute, of corse be discharged. If she bring actions against her calumniators, perhaps a little more spirit will be shewn[sic] on the side of the prosecution; - but, from henceforth we must hear no more complaints of the administration of justice.

Cleared of all charges, because no-one gave evidence. Although this news wasn't reported until January 13th, Ann had been released immediately after appearing in court the month before, on December 12th.

Although she wasn't found guilty of any statutory crimes, she was still classed as a vagrant, so she would have been sent back to her home parish of Nichol Forest.

Ann was quiet over Christmas and New Year, and I would guess she was very lucky in February 1788, when she was charged at Penrith with stealing printed calicoes – but was acquitted.

Everything seemed quiet until August 1788, when something just a little unbelievable happened at Carlisle assizes.

There is a brief report of the days' cases, with a number of people being charged for various reasons. A single line in the middle of the report says:

Ann Greggs, alias Hamilton, for making her escape from Carlisle gaol in the year 1786, where she was confined for felony; acquitted, and discharged.

Acquitted, then discharged? How on earth did she manage that? She was obviously in gaol at that time – newspaper reports and the gaoler's petitions prove that. It was also well-reported that she broke out – yet, here she is – acquitted! Could she have confused the judge, just as she had already confused me – and led him to believe she was a different Ann Gregg? Or did this uncanny woman have some kind of a hold over the magistrate? One can only speculate.

Things go pretty quiet on the crime front, as far as she is concerned. Or at least, as far as I can tell. Perhaps Ann couldn't believe her luck at being acquitted for breaking out of gaol and decided to behave herself for a while. Or perhaps she was just busy at home with her husband William and having another son, John, in 1790; then twins, Ann and Jane, in 1792.

But just to keep me on the ball, she makes a surprise appearance during her pregnancy with the twins, when she is back in Carlisle goal on suspicion of theft and declaiming in great distress that her husband is being transported. This can't be true, because her husband, William Hutchinson, is still around and he fathers another child a couple of years later, in 1794.

This is what the newspaper reported.

Newcastle Courant January 21st, 1792

Tuesday, Mr Mullender, his Majesty's Gaoler in Carlisle, accompanied by his son, set off for Portsmouth in the heavy coach, with ten convicts, for Botany Bay, by order of the Right Hon. Henry Dundas, one of his Majesty's principal Secretaries of State.

One of these unfortunate men is the nominal husband of the celebrated Ann Gregg, whose character in the North of England is too well known. She is at this time under confinement in the same gaol, upon suspicion of stealing a truss of goods, the property of Mess. Forster's, in Carlisle. The parting between her and the husband, had so great an effect upon her tender feelings, that it threw her into a most violent hysterics, which continued without any intervals for some time.

This is the most confusing report I'd come across, leaving lots more questions than answers. Having searched the gaoler petitions, I found no claim for any expenses for removing ten prisoners to be transported. And convict records for transports from Cumberland reveal nothing. This is very curious.

And "nominal husband" is an interesting use of words. Does it suggest that it wasn't Ann's husband William she was referring to, but her lover? I doubt it. Ann was pregnant at the time with twins, Ann and Jane. They were later baptised at Cumwhitton, Carlisle, on July 22nd, 1792, with William clearly stated as their father.

Jane and Ann Twin Daughters of William Hutchinson of [illegible] Bridge, Tinker and Ann his wife formerly Gregg.

So, either the report was wrong on several counts – there doesn't seem to be any evidence I can find that there were convicts being transported, and it wasn't Ann's husband. Or, the transportation involved another gang member and Ann was involved in some scam – pretending to be the convict's pregnant common-law wife, unconsolably hysterical that he was being transported; perhaps in the hope that he would be allowed to stay. This situation was certainly causing me even more confusion. I can only surmise it was another of Ann's smokescreens.

And then she goes and does it again.

Cumberland Paquet 10th April 1792

TWO FELONS ESCAPE FROM JUSTICE

Carlisle 3rd April 1792

BROKE out of Carlisle gaol, in the night of the said instant, ANN GREGG, alias ANN HAMILTON, alias ANN RITCHIE [that's a new one!] and JANE DIXON. Is about 5 feet 6 inches high, of a Sandy complexion, sandy coloured hair, left eye is blood-shot, speaks the Border dialect, and is known in most parts of the North of England. She had on a long grey cloak, and had in her possession a bundle of Muslins &c for sale.

The said JANE DIXON is about 5 feet 1 inch high, of a fair complexion, pitted with the Small-Pox, has a sharp nose, grey eyes and light coloured hair. She had on a dark cotton Bed-Gown, and Black Gown.

A Reward of FIVE GUINEAS and all reasonable expenses is offered to any person, or persons, who will apprehend either of the said felons, and deliver them to the Keeper of the Gaol at Carlisle; or Lodge them in any of his Majesty's Gaols, and give notice thereof.

Yet again, she had broken out of gaol! Either heavily pregnant with twins, or recently having given birth.

However, it seems that Ann had really cooked her goose this time. FIVE GUINEAS

REWARD was a small fortune in those days, and it shows how serious the situation was becoming. She had a price on her head, and it was a significant sum that meant someone *really* wanted her brought to justice. Rewards were paid by local "well-to-do" citizens such as magistrates, judges, landed gentry and business owners. Perhaps by now they had all simply had enough.

Only eleven days after her escape, it was reported, in romantic, melodramatic style:

Cumberland Paquet 14th April 1792

The celebrated Mrs. Ann Gregg, alias Ann Hamilton, alias Ann Ritchie, made her escape from Carlisle on the night of the said instant. She was committed on the 29th of October, charged with stealing checks, &c. from Messrs. Forster and Sons, and is now travelling the country (it is said) as a muslin dealer. Another lady, a Miss Jane Dixon, also took her departure on the same night. No hero of romance was ever more famous for dissolving the spells which bound unfortunate ladies in enchanted castles, than Mrs. Gregg is for finding the way out of modern jails and houses of correction, with most of which, in the North of England, she has for years past been exceedingly well acquainted: She has now, contrary to all expectations, added another instance to the former notable proofs of her knowledge in that particular, - see the advertisement.

That's almost poetic. In my mind, and I'm sure in some local circles, she has become something of a folk hero. I like the way she is described as "celebrated" – again.

"No hero of romance was ever more famous." She had clearly captured the public imagination and was better known than the leading character or hero of any novel. I suspected she was notorious, but is this really the Ann Gregg we know ?

"Dissolving spells which bound unfortunate ladies in enchanted castles." I know that journalists of the day were given to overly dramatic creative flourishes, but this really takes the biscuit. It is, however, a magical image that makes me smile.

You can't help but warm to her; at the same time as wondering what she's going to get up to next!

So, she had once again escaped from prison. But wheels keep on turning, and the next time, it was serious.

Ann Greggs, alias Ann Hutchinson, (She is exceedingly well known by the former name) was tried and convicted of petit larceny, and ordered to be transported for seven years.

That was it. A short and sweet report on the proceedings at Cockermouth Sessions on the 13th of January. It was stated that:

"There was the greatest number of Magistrates (12) upon the bench at Cockermouth on Monday ever remembered," chaired by James Clarke Satterthwaite.

I wondered if they were all there to see off their old adversary.

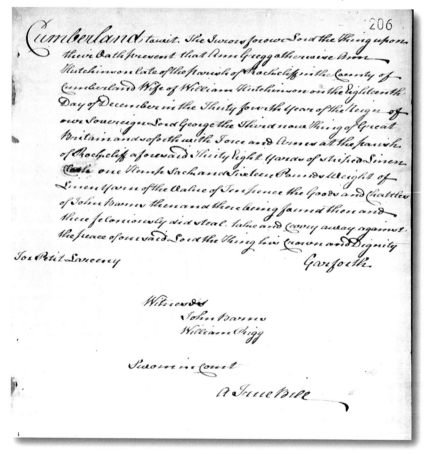

Ann Gregg's Examination

80

The Court case deposition stated:

Cumberland, to wit.

The Jurors for our Lord the King upon their oath present that Ann Gregg otherwise Ann Hutchinson, late of the parish of Rockcliffe in the County of Cumberland, Wife of William Hutchinson, on the eighteenth day of December in the thirty fourth year of the Reign of our Sovereign Lord George the Third now King of Great Britain and so forth, with force and Arms at the parish of Rockcliffe aforesaid thirty eight yards of striped linen cloth, one hemp sack and sixteen pounds weight of linen yarn of the value of Ten pence, the goods and chattels of John Barns then and there being found, then and there feloniously did steal, take and convey away against the peace of our said Lord the King his Crown and Dignity.

For Petit Larceny   *Garforth*

Witnesses

             John Barns
             William Prigg

Sworn in Court

                 A Truebill

They'd finally got her. No major headline, no big story in the newspaper. I had imagined that when her luck finally ran out, she would go out in a blaze of glory; but no – just a couple of lines in the local newspaper. And that was the end of Ann Gregg's criminal career.

Chapter 14
1793 - James Gregg.

As you might recall, Ann's brother, James Gregg, married Jenny Hutchinson at the same place and on the same day as William and Ann. It seems that one brother and sister married the other sister and brother.

James and Jenny Gregg had a son, John, who was baptised at Nichol Forest on 27th April, 1784.

I wondered if it was a case of "like sister, like brother" – had James Gregg got up to any mischief? It didn't take long to search the newspaper archives and find:

Newcastle Courant 15th December 1792

James Gregg, butcher, (brother to the noted Ann Gregg) and James Smith, were committed to Carlisle gaol, the 29th ult. charged with stealing two wedder sheep, the property of Mr. Stalker of Lamsfield, near that city.

There was absolutely no doubt this was the person I was looking for. James had stolen two wedder sheep – castrated males – more than likely to feed his family. With what seemed to be typical Gregg humour, he'd given his occupation as "butcher". To me this is James making fun of his crime, where he had "butchered" the stolen animals. His occupation on the indictment was labourer.

James had been taken before the Justices of the Peace, Brown Grisdale, Doctor in Divinity, and Thomas Forster, Esquire, on November 20th, 1792 and examined. His accuser, William Stalker, of Lambsfield Farm, near Dalston, gave his account first.

William Stalker

Who Saith that he had a quantity of sheep, depastureing in a field called Wettclose adjoining Broadfield in the Parish of Dalston in the County aforesaid and that two of the said sheep in the night of Friday the 23rd Day of November instant, or early in the morning of Saturday the 24th Day of the same Month, were feloniously stolen, taken and carried away from the said field so called Wettclose as aforesaid. That in consequence of the said sheep so being stolen, he the informant, together with Robert

82

Cumberland. To wit. The Examination of William Stalker of Lambfield in the said County Yeoman, Taken upon Oath before us Browne Grisdale Doctor in Divinity and Thomas Forster Esquire, two of his Majesty's Justices of the Peace in and for the said County this 28th Day of November 1792 ————

————————————— Habitation. ———

Who Saith that he had a Quantity of Sheep ————— depasturing in a Field called Wittclose adjoining Broadfield in the Parish of Dalston in the County aforesaid, and that two of the said Sheep, in the Night of Friday the 23d Day of November instant, or early on the Morning of Saturday the 24th Day of the same Month, were feloniously Stolen, taken and carried away, from the said Field so called Wittclose as aforesaid That in consequence of the said Sheep so being Stolen he this Informant, together with Robert Jefferson, Thomas Jefferson, William Mitchell, and Nathaniel Bailey, searched the Dwelling House, outhouses, and Gardens, of James Gregg of Bowrainshill, in the Parish of Sebergham in the said County Labourer, for the said Sheep, and that in the Garden of the said James Gregg, they found, two Skins, of two Sheep buried therein with the whole or part of the Carcase, or Carcases, contained in a Tub, which said Tub the Wife of the said James Gregg owned and acknowledged, to be her Tub, Saith that the Carcase, or Carcases contained in the said Tub, were then warm and that the said two Skins, together with the said Carcase or Carcases, so found as aforesaid, are the Property of him this Informant; one of which said Skins Marked 18 is one of the Skins, which was on one of the Sheep so Stolen and the Property of him this Informant Saith that he also found two Heads of two Sheep, under the Bed, of the said James Gregg which he was then lying on, Wherefore this Informant hath Just Cause to suspect and doth suspect that the said James

The Deposition of William Stalker

83

Jefferson, Thomas Jefferson, William Mitchell and Nathaniel Bailey, searched the Dwelling house, outhouses and gardens of James Gregg of Barranshill, in the Parish of Sebergham in the said County, labourer, for the said sheep, and that in the Garden of the said James Gregg, they found two skins of two sheep buried therein with the whole or part of the carcass or carcasses contained in a Tub. Which said Tub the Wife of the said James Gregg owned and acknowledged to be her tub. Saith that the Carcass or Carcasses contained in the said tub were then warm and that the said two skins together with the said Carcass or Carcasses so found as aforesaid are the Property of him this informant, one of which said skins Marked IS is one of the Skins which was on one of the Sheep so Stolen and the Property of him. This informant Saith that they also found two heads of two sheep under the Bed of the said James Gregg which he was lying on, Wherefore this Informant hath just cause to suspect and doth suspect that the said James Gregg feloniously did Steal and Carry away the same.

James's answer to his accuser wasn't very comprehensive.

James Gregg

Who Saith that he knows nothing of the felony of which he stands charged with.

The case wasn't heard until the Michaelmas assizes, when it was reported:

Newcastle Courant 10th August 1793

At the Assizes at Carlisle, one of the notorious Greggs, who has so long infested the County of Cumberland, was found guilty of sheep stealing, and received sentence of death.

A death sentence! That was horrifying to read. And as for calling the Greggs notorious – that sounded about right. But "infested" is worse – suggesting vermin. A pretty appalling term, indicative of their attitude towards gypsies and their kind.

I was glad to see that the report in the Cumberland Paquet made slightly better reading.

The Assizes - ended at Carlisle, on Wednesday. To the credit of the county, there were few felons to try. - James Gregg, convicted of stealing two sheep, the property of William Stalker, received sentence of death, but was reprieved before the judge left the city. Gregg's sentence is changed to transportation for life.

That was a relief. As bad as transportation must have been, it had to be better than the gallows.

A judge's report stated:

At the City of Carlisle {and for the County of Cumberland} 2nd August 1793

James Gregg of sheep stealing to be transported beyond the seas to such place as your Majesty with the advice of your Privy Council shall order and direct for the term of his natural life.

He was tried before me,
M MacDonald

Thank goodness for that. I really didn't want a hanging in the family.

On the 12th of September, a letter of disposal was signed. This was to remove James from Carlisle gaol and transport him to a prison hulk on the Thames while he waited for his order of transportation.

Whitehall 12th September 1793

Justices of Assizes for the northern circuit. Gent.

The following persons having been tried and convicted before you at the last assizes holden on the northern circuit of the crimes hereafter mentioned Viz.

David Andsley at the Castle of York for Burglary

Edward Banks of the same place of Sheep stealing

Isabel Robson at Newcastle upon Tyne for the County of Northumberland of Burglary.

Robert Musgrave of the same place of Highway Robbery and

James Gregg at Carlisle for the County of Cumberland of Sheep stealing.

And you having by Certificate under your hands humbly recommended them to the King as fit object of the Royal mercy on Condition of their being Transported beyond the seas for the terms hereafter mentioned Viz.

Said Robert Musgrave for the term of Seven Years and the said David Andsley, Edward Banks, Isabel Robson and James Gregg for and during the term of their natural lives, His Majesty has thereupon been graciously pleased to extend his Royal Mercy to the said several persons on Condition of their being transported for and during the terms above mentioned to the Eastern Coast of New South Wales or some one or other of the islands adjacent and has Commanded me to signify the same to you that you may give the necessary directions accordingly.

I am
Henry Dundas

James is sentenced to death, then receives the King's royal mercy on condition that he is transported for life. I wonder if the King had any idea what life in the colonies was like, and which fate may be the worst?

A Petition put before the Carlisle Quarter Sessions at Michaelmas, 1794 is very interesting.

Carlisle Sept.

To Conveying 6 Transports, namely James Gregg, John Sewell, Henry Routlege, Thos. Rutherford, Violet Chambers, Ann Hutchinson from Carlisle to London being 308 miles at 1s per mile ….

£90.6s.0d

To conveying 4 Transports, namely James Gregg, John Sewell, Henry Routlege, Thomas Rutherford from London to Woolwich being 12 miles at 1s per mile.

£2.8s.0d

£92.14s.0d

Two years after being arrested and one year after his conviction, James had been sent to London at the same time as his sister. What a coincidence! Or is this something else that Ann manipulated?

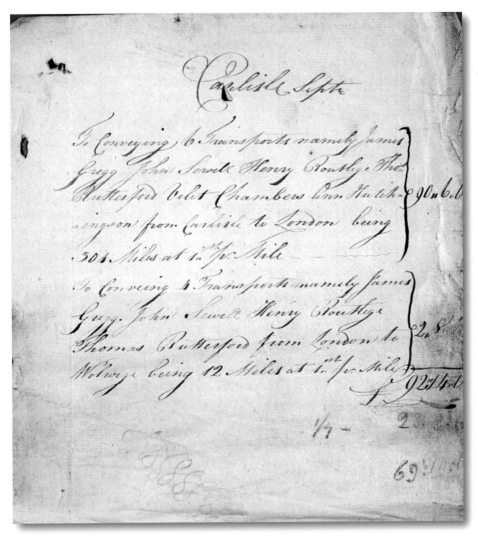

Costs of transport from Carlisle to London

And there was Violet Chambers, the dapper little captain, again!

The next document I found was undated, but it must have been from while he was in gaol, prior to transportation. The document is a list of names of convicts, where they were convicted, when convicted, term of sentence and the name of the vessel the convict would be transported on. Interestingly, there is no vessel listed for James.

But what caught my attention was the line below James: "Gregg, Sarah, alias Hutchinson". Who was that?

There were no entries showing where and when she was convicted, and no term of sentence, but *Britannia 3* was the vessel listed. There had to be a connection between James and Sarah. Australian convict records are pretty comprehensive, and I've found the list of convicts who were transported on *Britannia 3*. There isn't any record of a Sarah Gregg/Hutchinson.

An e-mail to the N.S.W. archives in Australia brought the response that it was probably just "an error". Knowing Ann as I do, now, it was more likely to be a case of Ann causing confusion, yet again.

A very interesting petition was sent to the Duke of Portland on March 17th 1795. James and another convict John Gray who were both being held on the prison hulk "Stanislaus" at Woolwich, were asking to be transported on the next available ship. John Gray claimed to be a carpenter, James had now changed from being a butcher to a stone mason, who "flatters himself that he would be useful to the colony".

This was clearly a ruse, intended to get them sent to their inevitable destination, rather than continue languishing in the dreadful conditions onboard hulks. The petition didn't seem to work and their incarceration continued. It was more than a year later when James next appears on an indenture dated 9th August, 1796, to be transported to New South Wales on board the *Ganges*. The indenture was a contract between Thomas Shelton – who was Clerk to the Court of Arraigns, Clerk of the Peace and Coroner to the City of London – and the ship's captain, Thomas Patrickson. The contract was to transport James Gregg from gaol to the ship, and on the ship from London to New South Wales. More correctly called ships' musters, they were like an early form of passport.

The *Ganges*, a 700-ton merchantman: a three-tier ship, had been built in India and was launched in 1794. She had previously been chartered to the East India Co. and was now commissioned to transport convicts to Australia. She arrived in Portsmouth on 15th October, 1796, taking on board rations and supplies in preparation for the voyage. She was to transport 194 convicts who were being held in prison hulks on the Thames, plus other convicts who would embark in Ireland.

Ship's surgeon, James Mileham, was entrusted with the convicts' and crew's health. The *Ganges* was one of the first convict ships to be inspected by Sir James Fitzpatrick, the Home Department's Surgeon General. He reported to the Under Secretary of State John King:

To His Grace the Duke of Portland
His Majestys Principal Secretary
of State.
                The humble Petition of
John Gray and James Gregg Convicts
On Board the Stanislaus hulk Woolwich.

Sheweth
                That Your humble Petitioner John
Gray was Convicted at Nottingham Assizes
March 1793. And Recd. Sentence to be Transported
For his natural Life And being by Trade a
Carpenter humbly Implores your Graces humanity
That he may be Sent to his place of destination
In one of the First Ships destind to carry Convicts

                That Your humble Petitioner James
Gregg was Convicted at Carlisle In Augt. Assizes 1793
And Recd. Sentence to be Transported for his
Natural Life And being by Trade a Stone Mason
Flatters himself he may be Usefull to the Colony
Humbly Prays your Graces Interference that
He may be sent in one of the First Ships
Destind to carry Convicts And Your Graces
Humble Petitioners Shall In duty bound ever pray

        John Grey Aged 33 by Trade a Carpenter
        James Gregg Aged 30 by Trade a Stone Mason
                        Dated March 17th. 1795

James Greggs Petition to be Transported

89

Surgeon Fitzpatrick to Under Secretary King.

Sir, Portsmouth, 23rd October, 1796., ...

...Your manner of receiving me when embarked on the part of a poor miserable convict emboldens me to state to you, for his Grace the Duke of Portland's information, the matters which have been done here, and those which I pray may be done at Cork, for Health of the accommodation and health of the convicts embarked onboard the Ganges. My first object was, in as much as the mode of the original fitting of the ship would allow, to favour the perpetual admission of as much pure air as possible.

Then it became my concern to pay that attention to the poor women, which their conduct deserved, by placing them under the protection of their husbands, their merit in a conjugal sense being nearly unparalleled, sacrificing their all, and subjecting themselves to an ignominious banishment, thereby fulfilling the great and essential obligation of the marriage vow.

The Ganges

I railed off a part of the vessel where the convicts were confined and allotted it to the married men, their partners, and innocent orphans. By this alteration, the poor women, in place of being subject (as they were before) to the insult of the ship's crew and the military guard, are now protected, and the space which they inhabited is now converted into an hospital apartment, well aired. I put on board ventilators and water-purifiers, also vitriol and nitre for fumigation, and such medicines as were required by Mr. Mileham.

His recommendations and changes were quite revolutionary, in humanitarian terms; making that ship safer and healthier than most prison transportation ships had been, to date.

The *Ganges* departed from Portsmouth on 10th December, 1796, in the company of the *Britannia*, calling at Ireland to take on more convicts. The ship's guards were soldiers of the New South Wales Corps, consisting of two officers and sixty private soldiers.

During the voyage, there were thirteen deaths. The *Ganges* arrived in Port Jackson, Australia, on 2nd June, 1797.

Lieutenant-Colonel Collins provides a little more insight into the journey.

On the 2nd of June, the ship Ganges arrived from Ireland, with convicts from that kingdom, and a detachment of recruits for the New South Wales corps. This ship had touched at the Cape of Good Hope, and was commanded by Mr. Patrickson, who had visited the settlement in the year 1792, in the Philadelphia, a small American brig. The convicts in this ship were observed to be in much better health than those on board of the Britannia. These people, indeed, complained so much of having been treated with great severity during the passage that the governor thought it right to institute an enquiry into their complaints. It appeared that they had been deserving of punishment, but that it had been administered with too much severity, in the opinion even of the surgeon who was present. As these punishments had been inflicted by the direction of the master, without consulting any of the officers on board as to the measure of them, he was highly censured, as was the surgeon, who could stand by and see them inflicted without remonstrating with the master, which he declined because he had not been consulted by him.

Whilst conditions on the ship were healthier and the family units were allegedly kept safer, it is apparent that any punishment that was meted out onboard was extreme and excessive, and the surgeon, whilst deeming it too severe, had stood by and watched, and had not intervened, simply because he hadn't been consulted about it. At least their cruelty was acknowledges, but that's no help to the suffering of those who had been tortured and died at the master's sadistic hands.

After the long sea journey, the process for disembarkation was not a simple procedure.

Upon arrival in a convict colony, port regulations forbade all but the ship's surgeon superintendent to go ashore, until permission was formally granted by the Colonial Governor. Presumably, they would be assuring the authorities that the ship wasn't bringing infectious diseases likely to cause epidemics onshore, or to prepare for the quarantine of anyone ill.

It was the surgeon who conveyed the indenture to the Governor and with it, gave him control of the convicts, The Governor, in turn, deposited it in the Colonial Secretary's office. There, it provided the sole colonial proof of an individual's status as a transported felon. Their name and the ship they arrived on were key to their identification and were used on all future documents. The indenture was a crucial part of the process of shipping out convicts to the penal colonies, both practically and legally.

The Colonial Secretary then passed the indentures on to the Muster Master, who was charged with constructing two large ledgers of information: one volume to be held in the colony, and the other to be returned to Britain. Immediately, the Muster Master began by transcribing information from the indenture onto very large sheets, each convict occupying a single line across the page, where there were a series of columns. With other documents also available, he partially filled in his pages.

Then, within a day or two of landing, and before any convicts were allowed to disembark, the Muster Master, accompanied by the Principal Superintendent of Prisoners, would board the ship, armed with his prepared sheets to make a minute examination of every prisoner on board. Based on observation and interview, he filled in the remaining columns with personal descriptions of each and every convict. It is these documents, compiled by the Muster Master, that are today known as "convict indents". These documents can give us a great insight to the physical appearance of our ancestors, as they generally give their height, complexion, hair colour, eye colour and distinguishing marks. They can also refer to their religion, former convictions, level of literacy, marital status and number of children.

Although James had been sentenced to transportation for life, he can't have been seen as much of a threat to anyone. Or perhaps it was because he'd been given the King's mercy – but the next undated document in which James appears is an employment record, showing him working in Parramatta as a housekeeper. This was quite a privileged role – or a cushy number, compared to hard labour.

Convicts who had specialist skills fared the best in the colonies. In a new land that needed every kind of trade and skill to build the colony, people with some expertise and experience: shoe makers, tailors, sawyers, blacksmiths, etc. were top of the heap. Others were trained to make buckets and water barrels, build brick walls and cut down trees. The convicts like James, who could secure employment as a housekeeper – either for a freed convict or a settler – generally had easier lives.

From 1797 until 1804, there were no more signs of James, until I found a very interesting record – of the baptism of Sarah Gregg, daughter of James Gregg and Martha Anderson. James had a new family! I wonder what happened to his wife Jenny and son, John, whom he'd left back home?

His new wife, Martha Anderson, another convict from Alnwick, Northumberland, had arrived on the *Earl Cornwallis* on 12th June, 1801, along with one hundred and sixty-six male and eighty-seven female convicts.

Port Jackson

Francois Peron, a young naturalist on expedition with *Geographe* and *Le Naturaliste*, arrived at the same time as James.

His wonderful description of Port Jackson would have been exactly what the arriving convicts saw; although I doubt that they saw the scene in front of them through the same rose-tinted glasses.

Towards the middle of this magnificent port, and on its southern bank, in one of the principal creeks, rises Sydney Town, the capital of the county of Cumberland, and of all the English colonies in this part of the world; seated at the base of two hills, that are contiguous to each other and having the advantage of a rivulet, which runs completely through it; this infant town affords a view, at once agreeable and picturesque. To the right, and at the north point of Sydney Cove, you perceive the signal battery, which is built upon a rock, difficult of access; six pieces of cannon, protected by a turf entrenchment, cross their fire with that of another battery, which I shall presently mention; and thus defend, in the most effectual manner the approach to the harbour and the town. Further on, appear the large buildings that form the hospital, and which are capable of containing two or three hundred sick.

Amongst these buildings, there is one particularly worthy of notice, as all the parts of it were prepared in Europe, and brought out in Commodore Phillip's squadron; so that in a few days after its arrival, there was an hospital ready to receive such of the crews as were sick. On the same side of the town, at the sea shore, you observe a very fine magazine, to which the largest ships can come up, and discharge their cargoes. In the same direction are several private docks, in which are built brigs and cutters, of different sizes, for the purpose of trading either inland or beyond the colony. These vessels which are from fifty to three hundred tons burthen, are built entirely with the native wood; even their masts are obtained from the forests of the colony.

It is at the spot called Hospital Creek, that the ships of individuals unload their cargoes. Beyond the hospital in the same line is the prison, which has several dungeons capable of holding from an hundred and fifty to two hundred prisoners; it is surrounded by a high and strong wall, and has a numerous guard on duty, both by day and night. A short distance from the prison is the storehouse, for the reception of wines, spirituous liquors, salt provisions etc. In the front of it is the armoury where the garrison is drawn up every morning; accompanied by a numerous and well composed band, belonging to the New south Wales regiment.

The whole western part of this spot is occupied by the house of the lieutenant governor general; behind which is vast garden which is worth the attention both of the philosopher and the naturalists on account of the great number of useful vegetables which are cultivated in it; and which have been procured from every part of the world by its present respectable possessor, Mr. Paterson, a distinguished traveller, and member of the Royal Society of London. Behind the house and the magazine just mentioned is the public school; here are educated in the principles or religion morals and virtue, those young females who are the hope of the rising colony; but whose parents are either too degenerate or too poor to give them proper instruction. In the public school, however, under respectable matrons, they are taught from their earliest years all the duties of a good mother or a family.

Behind the house of the lieutenant governor in a large magazine, are deposited all the dried pulse and corn, belonging to the state. It is a sort of public granary intended for the support of the troops and the people who receive their subsistence from the government.

The barracks occupy a considerable square, and have in front several field pieces; the edifices for the accommodation of the officers form the lateral parts or ends of the building; and the powder magazine is in the middle. Near this, in a small private house, the principal civil and military officers assemble. It is a sort of coffee house, maintained by subscription, in which there are several amusements but particularly billiards, at which any person may play, free of expense. Behind the armoury is a large square tower, which serves for an observatory to those English officers who study astronomy.

On 13th April, 1812, James Gregg obtained his ticket of leave, which he had to carry at all times. This allowed him to work for himself, provided he remained in a specific area. He would also have had to report to his local authorities on a regular basis and attend church every Sunday. He would not have been allowed to go out of the colony.

On the 20th December of the same year, James petitioned the Governor, Lachlan Macquarie, to grant him emancipation. One month later, on 31st January 1813, James was granted a conditional pardon. He could start to build a life for himself. Ten years later, on 30th June, 1823, James took out a twenty-one year lease on a piece of land in Parramatta.

James and Martha's daughter, Sarah Gregg, grew up and married another convict, James Bardsley, a Lancashire weaver, who arrived onboard the *Morley 2* in 1817. James Bardsley and Sarah were married on 10th September, 1821, at St James's Church, Parramatta. This James also took a twenty-one year lease on land in Parramatta, on the same day as his father-in-law in 1823.

James Bardsley was granted his certificate of freedom on 22nd January, 1824. The 1828 census shows James and Sarah Bardsley, along with their servant girl, fifteen-year-old Elizabeth Gorman, living at Bardsley's farm, a 50-acre property at Parramatta. Only 10 acres of that were cleared and cultivated, according to the records, and they apparently had 5 horned cattle.

All seemed to be going well. Until 10th August, 1837, when James Bardsley fell foul of the law again – and was convicted for receiving stolen goods. James received the worst possible sentence: his freedom was revoked, and he was transported to Norfolk Island.

Said to be a hell-hole in paradise, Norfolk Island was settled by Europeans on 6th March, 1788, when the British flag was raised by Lieutenant Philip Gidley King. The island was settled because of its strategic position, as well as the abundance of flax and high-quality timber growing there. The established colony on Norfolk Island gradually reduced from 1805 onwards, until it was finally abandoned in 1814. With the exception of pirates, who used it as a base from time to time, the island was uninhabited until 1825, when it was resettled.

Just over a decade later, Norfolk Island had become the most notorious penal station in the English-speaking world. In 1840, Charles Dickens even offered to write a short novel about it. His idea was to try to ensure that the lower classes held it in sufficient dread that it would act as a deterrent to crime. The island was considered a place to send the worst description of convicts. Its remoteness, seen previously as a disadvantage, was now viewed as an asset for the detention of "twice-convicted" men, who had committed further crimes since arriving in New South Wales. Normally, double offending prisoners who had committed non-violent crimes were sent there for three years and I'm presuming this was the punishment James received.

The last record I have for James is another certificate of freedom issued on 26th July, 1844. So, at least he made it that far.

So much for Ann's brother and his family. Let's get back to Ann. For that, we need to backtrack to the time when she and her brother were both about to be transported. 1794.

Chapter 15
1794 - Ann is Sentenced

Ann was sentenced to be transported to the colonies or plantations on the 13th January, 1794. She was thirty-nine years old and had been a habitual criminal for most of her life. In fact, she was lucky to have had a life at all, after being sentenced to death in 1777. Fortunately for Ann, that sentence had been commuted to three years in gaol.

With other Transports I'd researched, the story from their sentence onwards generally followed the same pattern.

(1) Sent to London.

(2) Held in gaol (or prison hulk, if a male) waiting to be shipped.

(3) Shipped.

(4) Arrived.

(5) Worked out sentence.

(6) Tried to carve out a new life in a new world.

That was pretty much the route her brother, James Gregg, had taken. I imagined the same for Ann.

Ann was sent from Carlisle gaol to Newgate gaol, London, with 5 other convicts, including her brother, James, and her friend, Violet Chambers.

The men were sent another 12 miles onwards, to Woolwich, where they would have been held on prison hulks, waiting for their transportation ship.

Female convicts were not held on hulks, so Ann and Violet Chambers were sent to Newgate. This would normally be their final home in England, before being transported.

Newgate Prison was a dismal, unhealthy place. Every year, approximately thirty people died there. Physicians often refused to enter the prison and people passing by held their noses. It was the oldest, most famous, and one of the most important prisons in eighteenth century England. Although it was technically a local prison under the control of the Lord Mayor and Aldermen of London, it held a special position, because it was not only the place of detention for all those awaiting trial at the neighbouring court, but it was also a sort of holding pen for those awaiting execution and transportation.

Newgate Prison

Documents show that Ann and Violet were initially sent from Carlisle to Newgate prison, where they were held for the next 80 days, at a cost of sixpence per day. They were then transferred to Giltspur Street Compter. Moving out must have been a relief, since conditions in Newgate were legendary.

Giltspur Street Compter was located close to Newgate Prison and was built in 1791 in order to replace the Poultry Compter and Wood Street Compter. It was designed to hold 136 prisoners. The prisoners were divided into four classes: debtors, felons, petty offenders, and those charged with assault. There were rows of cells for felons, separate buildings for male and female debtors, and separate rooms for those apprehended by the night watch. Despite the aspiration to keep prisoners divided by classification, in practice, inmates were moved around the prison regardless of their class, according to the space available. Giltspur Street must have felt like a five-star hotel to Ann and Violet after their short stay at Newgate.

Ann and Violet were indented to be transported on board the convict ship *Indispensable*, which was scheduled to sail on the 22nd October, 1795.

Ann's petition for clemency

It was normal for convicts being transported to have pleas for clemency made on their behalf. Although I've never found copies of any plea for Ann, one must have been made, because I found a copy of a reply, written by James C. Satterthwaite, the judge who presided over her indictment.

Papcastle, Sept 6, 1795

My Lord,

I am honoured with your Grace's letter enclosing the petition of Ann Gregg alias Hutchinson, who was convicted at the General Quarter Sessions held for the County of Cumberland at Christmas 1794 on the clearest evidence. I have enclosed a copy of the Bill of Indictment found by the Grand Jury. The facts therein found were fully proved upon the trial from the most minute inquiry, I find her general character is such, as in my opinion, not to make her a proper object of the Royal mercy.

I am your Lordship's most obedient servant,

James Satterthwaite

That doesn't take much explaining. She was beyond the point of no return. Ann's place on the *Indispensable* was booked, the date of departure set, Ann's plea was refused – so, that should have been that.

But this is Ann Gregg we're talking about, and we should never underestimate her ingenuity.

The ship sailed on 22nd October as planned, but Ann and Violet weren't onboard.

On the 29th October, Thomas Shelton had written at the end of the shipping indent:

"Be it Remembered that Ann Gregg otherwise Hutchinson, one of the female Convicts named in this Indenture and Contract, was not delivered to the within named Daniel Bennett."

Dated 29th day of October 1795.

Thomas Shelton.

Thomas Shelton was Clerk to the Court of Arraigns, Clerk of the Peace and Coroner to the City of London. It was his responsibility to enter into contracts with ships' owners to transport prisoners. Daniel Bennett was the Indispensable's owner and these few lines added to the end of the Indenture released Daniel Bennett from his contract to transport Ann.

I have never found any documents or references as to the reason Ann managed to avoid transportation. But once again for some uncanny reason, she managed to buck the system.

Ann and Violet were returned to the Compter, and records show that they they stayed for three years and eighty-nine days. This information was gleaned from documents held at Carlisle Archives. I saw that a bill had been sent to Carlisle (since they were from this County) asking for payment to Mr Newman, the keeper of Giltspur St Compter, the sum of £59 4s 0d each for Ann and Violet, for their maintenance over a period of 1184 days at 1/- per day.

The big question is: how did Ann and Violet manage to avoid transportation during the almost 3 1/2 years, they were held in the Compter?

Researching 18th century prison conditions and female transportation gave possible clues.

When a woman was convicted of a capital crime, she would be asked if there was any reason why a sentence of death or transportation should not be passed upon her. She could, at this point, "plead her belly," i.e. say that she was pregnant. A pregnant woman would never be executed, because it was considered immoral to kill an innocent baby.

The woman pleading her belly was often not sentenced to death or transported at this point, but was kept in prison and examined by matrons to see if she really was pregnant. Many of the claims of pregnancy were entirely baseless, since it was a great excuse in an attempt to avoid death or transportation. If the woman was found to be "quick with child," her sentence was delayed until after she'd given birth. Or alternatively, she was given a lesser punishment: her sentence could be commuted to transportation in the case of a death sentence; or to a prison sentence, in the case of transportation. If she was found not to be pregnant, she was returned to court to be formally sentenced, and then included in the next batch of executions or transports.

Anecdotal evidence suggests that women prisoners would sometimes try to get pregnant whilst in gaol to save themselves from the gallows or the ships. They would offer sex to other prisoners, their jailers or to visitors for this purpose. This was a last resort and to avoid their fate and the best thing they could do was to get pregnant.

So, did Ann or Violet become pregnant in prison? Did they give sexual or monetary favours (via gang members outside) to their gaolers in exchange for better conditions – that is, to be in the Compter, rather than stay in notorious Newgate? And did they give favours to keep off the transport lists?

There is absolutely no evidence at this stage, but these were two extraordinary women – and I believe they would have done whatever was necessary to stay healthy, alive and most importantly, in England.

I haven't been able to find any other relevant documents regarding details of their imprisonment, but I did find this correspondence from the High Sheriff of Cumberland to the Compter:

Sir

I am directed by His Grace the Duke of Portland to desire that you will forthwith provide for two female convicts in Giltspur Street Compter whose names are in the margin [Ann Gregg alias Hutchinson and Violet Chambers] the undermentioned articles of clothing

For each 2 spare shifts,

2 ditto pairs of stockings,

2 ditto handkerchiefs,

1 ditto pair of shoes,

I am sir,

Your most obedient humble servant,

High Sheriff of the county of Cumberland

J King

Ann and Violet were to receive some new clothes. I suppose they had been in gaol for almost four years. Prisons in the late 18th century didn't provide prisoners with clothing, these items had to be purchased from the Keeper. I doubt that either woman had any money, or if they did, it was being held back for more uncertain times.

The reason for the new clothes became apparent with another letter dated 15th January.

Whitehall 15 January 1798

Gentlemen, I am commanded to signify to you the King's pleasure that you do cause to be removed on board the Britannia Transport now lying in the River Thames without delay the several female convicts from Newgate and the New Compter named in the enclosed lists in order for transportation to New South Wales and that each convict be provided *with the undermentioned clothing agreeable to Mr King's letters of the 2nd and 6th instant, otherwise they will not be received on board.*

I am, Gentlemen,

Your most obedient humble servant,

Portland

There was a reply to the letter:

Sheriffs of London and Middlesex to

The High Sheriff of the County of Cumberland

Whitehall 15 January 1798

The names of two female convicts in the custody of Mr Newman, the Keeper of Giltspur Street Compter to be removed from that place on board the Britannia Transport bound for New South Wales in pursuance of the Duke of Portland's letter by the King's command dated 15th instant, directed to the Sheriffs of London and Middlesex and to the High Sheriff of the County of Cumberland.

1 Ann Gregg alias Hutchinson

2 Violet Chambers

To the High Sheriff of the County of Cumberland.

There was the answer: the women were to be shipped, on board *Britannia 3*, which was due to set sail on the 31st January, 1798 (*Britannia* actually sailed on February 17th). I was surprised, but it was to be expected. They had now served around four years of their seven-year sentence in English prisons. I'm not sure which they would have preferred – prison or colonies – if they'd been given the choice.

Being impatient, as I can be – I went straight to the Australian records and quickly found the ship's indent for Violet Chambers' arrival. It didn't take long until I'd found the same for Ann Gregg, alias Hutchinson. Their luck had finally run out. They had been sent "down under" at last.

Australian convict records are fairly extensive, and after researching several other convict transports, I'd learned to work my way through most of the online resources. But, try as I might, I couldn't find any record of them actually arriving

No	Names	Age	Where tried and when	Place of Transportation	Term
34	Ann Baker	40	Middx G.D. — 26 June 1796		
35	Mary Brown	28			
36	Mary Crawthorne	30	d° — 14 Sept. 1796		
37	Jane Richmond	39			
38	Ann Kennedy	40			
39	Catherine Fitzjohn	35	d° — 26 Oct. 1796		
40	Catherine Shepherd	30			
41	Sarah Jackson	40	d° — 30 Nov. 1796		
42	Ann Rochfort	16			
43	Mary Cordell	33	d° — 11 Jan. 1797		
44	Elizabeth Lewis	21			
45	Ann Croker	31	d° — 15 Feb. 1797		
46	Mary Smith als Warner	38			
47	Ann Hall	27	d° — 26 Apl 1797		
48	Mary Johnson	25			
49	Mary Bryant	20	d° — 31 May 1797		
50	Elizabeth Stirling	18			
51	Mary Bryan	16			
52	Sarah Draper als Ingram als Ann Walton	24		Bey.d the Seas	7 Years
53	Mary Cath Buckley	40	d° — 12 July 1797		
54	Ann Thompson als Bruce als Robinson	39			
55	Ann Dillon	40			
56	Elizabeth Allen	25			
57	Letitia Baker	24			
58	Elizabeth Meath	40	d° — 20 Sept. 1797		
59	Sarah McCann als Lloyd als Bevan	27			
60	Eleanor Carter	25			
61	Mary Ann Mowy	19	d° — 25 Oct. 1797		
62	Sarah Johnson	14			
63	Mary Valence	30			
64	Mgt Gill als Wilson	43	d° — 6 Dec. 1797		
65	Sarah Best als Catapudi als Brown	23			
66	Catherine Cody	38	Westminster Sess. — Jany 1795		
67	Mary Wise	20	d° — Oct. 1795		
68	Ann Jones	22	Salop G.D. 1st Augt 1795		
69	Margaret Edwards	27	d° — 25 March 1797		
70	Mary Patten	26	d°.2. Sess: 10 Jan. 1797	Col. or plant	d°
71	Eliz: Cely als Eliz: Kewer	19	Somerset G.D. 8 Augt 1795	bey.d the Sea	d°
72	Elis. Wife of Robert Vickary	40			14 Years
73	Mary Wife of Thomas Ford	24	d° — 2: Sess. 26 April 1797		
74	Rebecca Thomas	19			
75	Susannah Hendrick	50			
76	Frances Ferguson als Grosvenor als Frances Wife Cha.s Herbert Fox	26	Surrey G.D. 20 March 1797	d°	7 Years
77	Elizabeth Hill	27	Warwick G.D. 25 Mar. 1794	d°	14 Years
78	Mary Smith	24			
79	Sarah Cotterell	50	d° — 21 Mar. 1796	d°	7 Years
80	Mary Hide als Sarah Blunn	37			
81	Ann Gregg als Ann Hutchinson	50	Cockermouth Cumberland 2: Sess: 13 Jan. 1794	Col. or Plantations	7 Years
82	Violet Chambers	50	Carlisle — 2: Sess: 28 Apl 1794	d° — d°	7 Years
83	Mary Philpotts	22	Hereford. — 1794	beyond Seas	7 Years

Britannia Indent

in New South Wales, or living in the colonies. No musters, no applications for marriage, no pardons – which should have happened three years after arrival. There was nothing.

I went back over all my notes, copies of letters, documents and everything I had on Ann, checking the details. Then, I spotted something odd.

On the actual indent for *Britannia*, there was a list of all female convicts sent to New South Wales on 31st January, 1798. Numbers 5 and 6, under a heading of "Cumberland" from Giltspur St Compter, were the names Ann Gregg alias Hutchinson and Violet Chambers. Both were crossed through, with an asterisk beside the name. I wondered what that meant.

Eventually, I went back to the Australian arrival indents, which were very unclear and difficult to read. I looked closer. There appeared to be a short list of names with asterisks beside them, and I could just make out Ann's and Violet's names. Above the list was written, "The persons against whose names this mark appears * were not sent".

They'd done it again! I think I cheered! I definitely punched the air. I was elated. There was life in the old girl, yet. Ann wasn't prepared to lay down and die.

She had found a way to evade transportation twice! I bet not many other convicts could claim that. What a truly remarkable woman.

Eventually, I found the following letter:

Whitehall 19 January 1798

Sir

I am directed by the Duke of Portland to desire that you will not remove Ann Gregg alias Hutchinson and Violet Chambers from your custody in order for their voyage to New South Wales, His Grace considering them as unfit on account of their age and the short term of their sentences.

I am, sir

Your most obedient humble servant

J King

Copy to Mr Newman, Keeper of the Giltspur Street Compter.

So, there had been an appeal for leniency, citing age (she would have been in her early forties) and sentence-length (she had about 3 years left to serve). What happened to her next is a bit hazy. Charges were still being made by Giltspur

Street Compter to Carlisle gaol for the maintenance of Ann and Violet, up to October, 1798. At first, my guess was that they were then sent back to Carlisle, on or around that date.

Carefully deciphering and transcribing the complete file of documents held by Carlisle archives revealed an ongoing argument between John Addison Newman, the Keeper of Giltspur Street Compter, and Mr J Hodgson, treasurer for Carlisle gaol, regarding the expenses incurred by the women up to October 1798, when they should have been transported on the *Britannia*. It looks, to me, that there had been lots of confusion because they had been indentured twice, but never sailed.

One letter among the collection is dated 2nd February, 1801, the date that Violet was released. My thoughts now are that both women remained in the Compter until their release.

The final piece I found regarding Violet read:

George R

Whereas Violet Chambers was, at a general Quarter Sessions held at Carlisle in and for the County of Cumberland in April 1794, tried and convicted of petit larceny and was sentenced to be Transported Seven years for the same; We in consideration of some favourable circumstances humbly represented unto us in her behalf are graciously pleased to extend our Grace and Mercy unto her and to grant her our Free Pardon for her said crimes. Her will and pleasure therefore is that you cause her the said Violet Chambers to be faithfully discharged out of custody and for so doing this shall be your warrant given at the Court at St James's this 2nd day of February 1801 in the 41st year of his reign.

By his Majesty's command

Portland

Violet had been given mercy, pardoned and finally freed.

I've tried very extensively to search for any further information on her, after the free pardon. The only thing I've found is her burial at Arthuret, Cumberland on 31st January, 1815.

Ann Gregg should have been released slightly before Violet, since she had been convicted three months earlier. Unfortunately, to date, I've not been able to find any documents relating to her release.

Her son, James, who had been born in Carlisle gaol in 1794, was baptised on March 1st, 1801 at St Cuthbert's Church, Carlisle. I don't believe this coincidentally happened around the time of Ann's release. I believe it was arranged after she was pardoned, and that she attended.

From 1801, Ann just disappears. I've searched for her under all her aliases, and there's nothing in newspapers nor in prison documents. I've searched court petty sessions, quarter sessions and assizes records and drawn a blank.

I prefer to believe that she didn't die soon after being released but put up another smoke screen and went on to live a full life. She had endured her seven year sentence, managing to avoid transportation. She deserved some peace after all she'd been through.

A final twist in the tale.

Earlier, I mentioned that I'd never found out what happened to Ann's son, James, after Ann was transferred to London.

When I was searching through all the petitions to Carlisle Gaol, looking for any reference to Ann being transferred back there prior to her release, I found various references to James Hutchinson, "The County Child", or to "Ann Gregg's son".

I went back to the time when Ann was removed from Carlisle to London and I searched every quarter's petitions. And there it was: clear evidence that James had stayed in Carlisle Gaol for the whole time while Ann was in the Compter! There are monthly bills for his accommodation. Almost every quarter, as a growing lad, he gets a new pair of shoes or clogs, and quite often, new clothes. From 1798, there are quarterly bills for schooling. Young James was getting a roof over his head, being clothed, regularly fed, and receiving an education – all provided by the County Gaol. In the Easter accounts for 1801, which would cover the period when James was baptised, there is an entry for renting a coach and horses with a driver to take James to Penrith, to visit the bone setter. There is also the bill from the bone setter, charging the County Gaol for setting James's broken leg. I wonder how that happened? Following the petitions, there are bills for a spelling book and eventually quills, ink and writing paper. Young James could read and write,

January. (Christenings 1801)

4. 6 Mary, daughter of James and Sarah Holmes, of Botchergate —

11 ... son of William and Mary ...

11. Joseph, son of Thomas Milburn and Ann his wife, late ...

18. John, son of James Devlin and Isabella his wife, late Johnston.

22. Richard, son of Richard Moses, Mason, & of Elizabeth his wife, (late Lee, heretofore ...)

February

5. Thomas, son of James Irving, Calico printer, & of Elizabeth his wife, (late ...)

9 Esther, daughter of Robert Bickup, Cotton Spinner, & of Mary his wife, (late Atkin...)

15 Thomas, son of Robert Hetherington, Taylor, and ... his wife, (late ...)

17 Jane, daughter of John Biggs, Weaver, and of Mary his wife, (late Faulder)

22 ... son of George Barker, Labourer, and of Ann his wife, (late ...)

22 Hannah, daughter of John Bell, and of Hannah his wife, (late James...)

March

... William, son of John Richardson, Shoemaker, & of Elizabeth his wife, (late ...)

... George, son of George Metcalfe, a Servant, & of Mary his wife, (late ...)

... Joseph, illegitimate son of Mary Dalton, of Harraby Hill. —

14 James, son of William Hutchinson, born in the County Gaol in 1794, and of Ann his wife (late Gregg) (she being then a Prisoner for Felony.)

8 Eleanor & Thomas, Children of George Wilson, Hatmaker, & of Isabella his wife (late ...)

16 George, son of George Lamb, Calico Printer, & of Jane his wife, late Wann...

... George, illegitimate son of Margaret Little, of Carleton. —

... Robert, son of James Brown, of Trowbridge, & of Sybal his wife (late Stockridge)

... Robert, son of Robert Wildman, ... of Margaret his wife, (late Macclean)

22 Esther & Elizabeth, Daughters of Isaac Allcock, Shoemaker, & of Esther his wife, (late ...)

22 Thomas, son of Thomas Armstrong, of Burthwaite, Labourer, & of Sarah his wife, (late ...)

April

... William, son of Henry Wright, Weaver, & Mary his wife, (late Pearson) Born...

... John, son of Joseph Collin, farmer, & Mary his wife (late Frink) ...

... Mary, daughter of Thomas Burges, Taylor, & Margaret his wife (late ...)

... Sarah, daughter of John Holme, of Botcherby, and of Mary his wife, (late Corkmouth)

... Margaret, daughter of John Forster, of Blackal, & of Mary his wife (late ...)

... Eleanor, daughter of Thomas Barlow, a Soldier, & of Sarah his wife, (late ...)

May

... Elizabeth and Hannah, daughters of Joseph Hanson, of Brisco, & of Mary his wife (late ...)

... Agnes, daughter of David Johnston, Weaver, & Elizabeth his wife (late ...)

... Mary, daughter of Thomas Mills, Labourer, & Margaret his wife (late ...)

... William, son of William Gibson, of Brisco, and of Ann his wife (late ...)

... Thomas, son of John Sowerby, of Cotcoats, Labourer, & of Ann his wife (late ...)

James Hutchinson's Baptism Record

108

I've checked all the gaoler's petitions for references to James, right through to the Easter quarter of 1804, when suddenly, he disappears. This probably coincided with his tenth birthday. He'd been housed, fed, clothed and educated for 10 years. This must have been a great opportunity for James to make something better of his life. At 10 years old, James would have been considered old enough to work, and may have been apprenticed to one of the weaving mills in the town. My guess – and it is only a guess – is that because James was born in the County Gaol, which was in the parish of St Cuthbert's, he may have been given settlement in this parish. I'd like to think that being educated and able to read and write, James quickly worked his way up the ladder, eventually having a comfortable life. Hopefully future research may uncover more about his life.

Chapter 16
1803 - William Hutchinson.

Twenty years after marrying Ann Gregg – and after their enforced estrangement through prison, then her disappearance or death sometime after her release in 1801 – it seems that Ann Gregg's husband William Hutchinson had moved on with his life. He had moved to West Cumberland, and married a woman called Ann Irvin – or Irving.

Ann Irvin's first child with William Hutchinson was Jane. She was baptised at St Peter's Church, Camerton, Cumberland, on January 8th, 1804. This was followed in rapid succession by George, baptised on September 29th, 1805, and Mary Ann, baptised on February 4th, 1806. Again, we don't know their exact dates and places of birth, given the travellers' predilection for waiting until they travelled to a favourite church or waiting for a date they considered to be lucky or significant.

The children's father, William Hutchinson, is shown on the baptism records as being from Seaton and his occupation is basket maker. All three baptism records show William's wife as "Ann late Irvin". This suggestion of a previous or maiden name would normally indicate that they were now married, although no record of marriage has ever been found.

William's place of settlement was Rockcliffe, just to the north of Carlisle. Seaton, where he is stated as living on the baptismal records, is in West Cumberland. For William to be allowed to change his parish of settlement, he must have fulfilled certain conditions: he either had firm employment to go to there, or he must have been able to rent a house at a minimum rent of £10 per year.

It looks as if William moved to the west of the county at some time during the period when his first wife, Ann Gregg, was in prison. Two of his sons by Ann Gregg, Peter and William, appear in records as living in the west, so it's highly likely he moved there with all his children. Much later records show that William was a basket maker for a colliery. This might have been permanent employment and how he came to move there. It's also a worthwhile guess that he had family in the area who would help him to look after his children.

He doesn't seem to have lived a peaceful, happy ever after kind of life. I suppose after leading a life of crime with Ann Gregg, and now having an extended family to feed, it was inevitable that William would eventually get into trouble again.

William Hutchinson, for stealing wearing apparel from William Watson of Wyburn, to be publicly whipped and imprisoned for six months.

William must have been well-known to the Justices, to be sentenced to a public rather than private whipping. If, like his first wife, he used many aliases, I don't suppose we'll ever discover the extent of his crimes.

I think it's also fair to say that anyone married to William would, most likely, also become involved in crime. So, I started looking for his new wife, Ann Irvin, in court reports and news articles.

The first time I found Ann on record for this is in 1822, in the report of the County Quarter Sessions, in a later chapter.

But first, in that same year, I discovered more about another female relative of Ann Greggs – Elizabeth Reay – who took me on an interesting diversion.

Chapter 17
1822 - Elizabeth Reay

I haven't found any links to crimes perpetrated by Ann Gregg's brother, John, but his wife, Elizabeth Cunningham, made several appearances at Carlisle Assizes. In one particular instance in 1779, she was charged along with John Miller, James White and Christian Miller, for breaking open a shop. The family name Miller seems to crop up regularly with the Greggs.

John Gregg and Elizabeth Cunningham had a daughter, Elizabeth, who married a David Reay. David had one or two petty offences against him, but nothing of great note.

Things gets interesting again when it comes to their daughter, Elizabeth Reay, born in 1804, the grand-daughter of Ann Gregg's brother, John.

In 1822, at the age of only eighteen, Elizabeth, a milkmaid, was indicted to appear at the Cumberland Michaelmas Sessions at Penrith, charged with petty larceny. She was found guilty.

Cumberland Paquet 21st October 1822

Elizabeth Reay, alias Wreay, for stealing a pair of shoes at Edenhall - to be transported seven years. There were also three indictments against this person.

Petty larceny was the felonious taking of another person's property with a value of one shilling (5p in today's money) or less. Three offences of petty larceny carried a sentence of transportation.

It was also further reported in the same edition of the newspaper that:

Elizabeth Ray, alias Rea, was next put to the bar under three separate bills charging her with stealing wearing apparel, shoes &c to all of which she pleaded not guilty. She was put upon her trial on a charge of stealing shoes on 4th September last, the property of Thomas Nelson, who deposed (after the case had been opened by Mr. Armstrong) that he was a servant with Wm. Dawson of Edenhall, and that on 4th September last, between 6 and 7 o'clock in the morning, he took off a pair of shoes and put them into a hole in the stable. About 12 o'clock the same day, he missed them, and did not see them till that day week, in the possession of Jane Thompson, who now deposed that she lived at the Town Head of Penrith. On the 4th September, prisoner asked her to buy a pair of shoes, which she said belonged to a poor Irish boy.

Witness, on this representation bought the shoes - Edward Scott was there when she delivered the shoes up.

Edward Scott, constable, produced the shoes - they were sworn to by Nelson.

Isaac Wilson, deposed as to having made the shoes for Nelson.

The Jury immediately returned a verdict of guilty, and the court thought it unnecessary to proceed with the two other indictments, and she was acquitted on them. She was sentenced to seven years transportation.

The other charges, of which Elizabeth was acquitted, were stealing a blue duffle cloak to the value of ten pence, the goods and chattels of Margaret Stephenson, and one cotton muslin gown, one cotton muslin skirt and one cotton muslin spencer (shirt), of the value of ten pence, the goods and chattels of Mary Bond.

I later discovered that Elizabeth was probably pregnant at the time of her indictment, which could have been the fact that sealed her fate. At the time of Elizabeth's indictment, under the acts of the Poor Law, her parish was responsible for providing poor relief for the mother and her child. This was a tremendous burden on small rural parishes, as they would have to look after her and her baby. What often happened to young pregnant girls was that additional charges were trumped up, in order to have the girl transported. Having three petty larceny indictments against her, but being found guilty on only one charge was enough to see her off. Although the courts could not legally transport an innocent child, the mother could elect to take the child with her, or leave it behind with other family members. This relieved the parish of it's responsibility to pay poor relief.

I haven't been able to discover anything else about Elizabeth – until fourteen months later, when she appears on the *Brothers* ship's muster.

Elizabeth would have travelled from Carlisle gaol to Newgate, a distance of around 300 miles. The coach probably stopped at Lancaster to pick up another eleven female convicts on its way.

The following is an account of the conditions on the journey, and it references Elizabeth Fry, the well-known philanthropist and prison reformer who was born into a wealthy banking family and married into the Fry's chocolate family. She was commemorated on the British £5 notes produced from 2001-2016. for her work in tirelessly campaigning for and achieving prison reform. The inhumane conditions of the women travelling on the *Brothers* for transportation at that very time are described here:

There is in existence a list of the names of women received in irons, on board the Brothers, which sailed in 1823; it was taken down at the time, by direction of Mrs. Fry, in order that a representation might be made upon the subject to the Government. By this list, it appears that twelve arrived on board handcuffed. Eleven women from Lancaster were sent to the ship "iron-hooped round their legs and arms, and chained to each other. The complaints of these women were very mournful, they were not allowed to get up or down from the coach without the whole being dragged together; some of them had children to carry, they received no help, or alleviation to their suffering."

A woman from Cardigan travelled with a hoop of iron round her ankle, until she arrived at Newgate, where the sub-matron insisted on having it taken off. In driving the rivet towards her leg to do so, it gave her so much pain, that she fainted under the operation. She stated that during a lengthened imprisonment, she wore an iron-hoop round her waist; from that a chain connected with another hoop round her leg above the knee, from which a second chain was fastened to a third hoop round her ankle: in the hoop that went round her waist were, she said, two bolts or fastenings in which her hands were confined when she went to bed at night, which bed was only of straw.

This report holds the first evidence of female convicts being transported on the *Brothers* with children. It seems likely that Elizabeth may have given birth in prison, during the time between conviction and transportation. The big question is: did Elizabeth take her child to New South Wales with her?

The *Brothers*, a 425-ton ship built in Whitby, Yorkshire, departed from England on 5th December, 1823, under the charge of Master, Charles Motley, with Ship's Surgeon Superintendent James Hall looking after the welfare of crew, free passengers and convicts. On board there were fifty-six free passengers and eighty-nine female convicts.

Arriving in Port Jackson on Friday, 7th May, 1824, the voyage was far from incident-free. In the early part of the voyage, many women suffered sea-sickness. There were also cases of ophthalmia and catarrh and at least two births. Free passenger, Mrs. Butler, gave birth to a child on 17 February and Bridget Hanning, who was 44 years old, gave birth to her eleventh child on the 17th March. Two days later, the baby was found dead in its mother's arms. Other deaths that occurred included Mary Partridge, 21 years old, who had been pining for the mother she'd left behind. The six-year-old son of Mrs. Butler died, and Mr Butler later died, as well. Altogether, the surgeon's journal recorded five deaths. None of those were convicts.

The most disturbing event of the voyage took place on the 13th December, somewhere off Madeira, when there was an attempted mutiny. The subsequent enquiry found there to be no assault established by evidence for either the charges of mutiny, nor conspiracy, nor assault. The matter was dismissed.

However, the evidence makes interesting reading – and it even features Elizabeth Reay by name. Some of the testimonies from the Historical Records of Australia are reproduced in full below. Although this section is a lengthy quotation, and its content describes the same incidents with some repetition, it is intriguing to spot the differences as well as the similarities between different people's statements.

Overall, not even the official enquiry could determine that there was a real mutiny or conspiracy – or even that an assault took place. But see if you can judge what the truth is. These statements do give a vivid picture of the course of events from a number of different witnesses' perspectives.

The incidents on the night in question involve an alleged physical attack (even attempted murder) of Hall, the Ship's Surgeon, by some of the women in an apparently organised riot that also involved Meach, the First Mate.

The first statement is that of the alleged victim, himself.

The Information of James Hall, Esquire.

I am Surgeon Superintendent of the female Convict Ship, Brothers; we sailed from England on the 5th of December and arrived at Hobart Town on the 15th of April. On the evening of the 13th of December, Ann Mullin, Convict, informed me that the women were going to beat me. She whispered this to me as the prisoners were passing down to the prison; about two hours after that, Ann Wilson, convict, came to my cabin, greatly agitated, and told me there was a plot laid and that the women were going to murder me. Immediately after this, it was between 7 and 8 o'clock in the evening, I went down to the prison gate; the ship was at sea at this time, somewhere in the neighbourhood of Madeira. On entering the prison, I found it in darkness and great uproar prevailing; several voices exclaiming that Russel had put out the light, others saying, 'for God's sake, Mr. Hall, don't go forward, for they will murder you.'

I immediately called for lights to be brought; some were brought, but instantly put out again by the women in the prison; but, by aid of the lights before they were put out, I was enabled to proceed to half the length of the prison in search of Russel, the woman who was said to have put out the light. I found her seated, having on the dress of a woman of another County. I desired her immediately to go on deck; a convict named 'Reay' was standing near her; Russel refused to obey my orders. I then went on deck to procure the assistance of the first mate, Mr. Meach.

I returned to the prison with him, and laying hold of Russel's arm to force her from the seat, Mr. Meach had laid hold of her other arm, and advised her to go on deck. I failed in my endeavours to force her out of the prison. I desired Mr. Meach to take charge of her, whilst I went on deck to procure more assistance, the prison being still in darkness. Immediately on turning round to quit Russel, a scream was set up and I heard a rushing behind me. and someone cried out "give it the Bugger".

I received a blow on the back of my neck which made me reel forward and fall; I then received several blows and some kicks; having recovered myself I got out of the prison gate close to which I had fallen, Mr. Meach being still in the prison. Captain Motley, the Master of the Ship, and Mr. Gale, the second mate, and some of the seamen had already arrived at the prison gate: we seized the arm of a woman, and endeavoured to pull her out of the gate. She exclaimed to the convicts within "Haul away, Buggers, if you haul my arm off." She succeeded in getting clear of us.

Lights being now brought, we entered the prison, and received Information that six women had created the disturbance; their names were Anne Russel, Catherine McManus, Ellen Meadows, Lydia Gardner, Catherine Ryan and Elizabeth Reay; these women were taken out of the prison and secured.

These women have since confessed that they were concerned in this affray, and that it had been proposed to them by Mr. Meach on the afternoon of the same day to put out the prison light in the evening, When I went down to prayers, to give me a good beating and jump my "bloody" guts out. And he further told them, no doubt he would be the first person I should call down to assist me, but he would assist them, and told them he would give them a bottle of rum. I am also able to prove that the said Mr. Meach did assist in rescuing one of the convicts from me and Captain Motley, and that he has himself confessed he was engaged in the mutiny; that he had false keys, by which he had caused the gate to be opened, and had taken a prisoner to his cabin for the purpose of prostitution; and that he gave permission to three of the crew to go to the women, who were confined in the coal hole in the middle of the night, and that he frequently expressed his determination to throw me overboard during the first gale of wind or blow my brains out. I am also able to prove that he struck me on the back of the neck during the mutiny in the prison. I can also prove that Mr. Meach was seen preparing his pistols, on or about the time he said he would blow my Brains out, and therefore pray that justice may be done.

James Hall, R.N., Surgeon Supt. Sworn Before me at Hobart Town, this 17th April, 1824.

Evidence of Edward Rundle

Police Office, 27 May, 1824.

Edward Rundle, now Second Mate on board the Ship Cumberland.

I being sworn, deposeth, that, on the evening when the disturbance took place amongst the women on board, he was on his duty, and heard Mr. Meach's voice in the prison and heard Sarah Twithridge, one of the female convicts, say to Mr. Meach that it was all his fault, and heard a blow struck and Sarah Twithridge scream out; that he then saw a light brought into the prison from the fore part of the ship and the light was immediately put out. Saith that the same evening Mr. Meach came to him on the quarter deck, after deponent had served out the provisions, and told deponent that Mr. Hall had cut off Catharine Ryan's hair and said it was a damned rascally shame. Saith that, about 5 or 6 o'clock that evening. Mr. Meach said that there would be a disturbance in the prison amongst the women; that deponent then went forward and heard one of the women "We have five or Six," but this was spoken in an inquiry into jocular manner and deponent did not know what it meant. After disturbance was over and the women quiet, Mr. Meach asked him if he had been securing the women or not, that against deponent replied "No," that Mr. Gale had, and said it was a damned shame to confine any women in that manner. Saith that on reference to what had taken place in the prison, Mr. Meach said that he had hold of Cathrine McManus's arm and had dragged her from Captain Motley's arms, and Meach said that Mr. Gale had tried to stop her, when Meach said to Mr. Gale "let her go." And that Mr. Gale said, what had he come down there for; that Mr. Meach after this conversation went further forward, and Mr. Meach said that one of the girls had got him by the arm and Mr. Meach said it was him and the woman let him go; that Anne Wilson then brought a light from the hospital, and Mr. Meach said to Cathrine McManus " do you see that," and immediately Cathrine McManus knocked the light out of Anne Wilson's Hand, and called her names: that Mr. Meach said to deponent. " Do you suppose that I went down to quell the mutiny; No, I told them I was only come down to bustle amongst them and not to hurt them"; that Mr. Meach then said, "I have given the old "bugger" a Pett on the neck," meaning, as deponent supposed, Mr. Hall, and repeated the words "Old Bugger," and that he would feel it in the morning. Saith that he, deponent, came on deck at 12 o'clock the same night, and Mr. Meach came to him and said that Mr. Fell, Thomas Robinson and Charles Ward were down in the hold with the women, and that Mr. Gale was a dirty dog rascal and could not be trusted; that deponent reported this to Mr. Gale, and about 2 o'clock in the morning, deponent saith he saw the three men come out of the hold; the same three men that he had been told were in the hold; that he spoke to them and is certain that they were the same. Saith that he heard Mr. Meach, in conversation with Mrs. Hares, say that he would shoot Mr. Hall and would call him out as a Gentleman when he came to Port Jackson; and further heard Mr. Meach say that if it came on a dark night and a gale of wind that he would throw the old Bugger (meaning Mr. Hall) overboard.

Edward Rundle. Sworn at the Police Office, Sydney, the 27 of May, 1824,

Evidence of Matthew Gale

Matthew Gale, Chief Officer of the Ship Brothers, being sworn, deposeth, that on the night the disturbance took place amongst the women on board, he heard the cry of "Murder" and that they were murdering the Doctor; that deponent went below to do his best to quell the disturbance in the place where the women were confined; that Mr. Meach was down there before him; that all was dark and there was a great bustle and disturbance amongst the women, and the cries of murder in a woman's voice still continued, but doth not know who the woman was; that during the bustle they got one woman, named Cathrine McManus, to the prison door; that Captain. Motley had hold of her arm on the outside, and deponent, who was in the Inside, had also hold of her arm to get her out of the prison as she was one of the refractory women; that Mr. Meach was standing close by deponent and said to deponent, "Gale, why don't you let the woman go"; that deponent said he would not, and asked Mr. Meach what he supposed he came down there for; that Cathrine McManus called out, "clap on behind and haul away"; that Mr. Meach then put his foot against the prison door to prevent the woman from being hauled out, and the woman pulling very strong behind Captain Motley let go his hold of Cathrine McManus; that deponent was then in the Inside of the prison and kept his hold of her until he was dragged by the woman to the forepart of the main hatchway; that he then let go his hold of her. Saith that he heard a blow struck, but the Woman offered no kind of violence towards him. Saith that the cry of "Murder" was in a female voice and not from Mr. Hall. Saith he thinks he was told that night that the cry of murder was from a woman named Russel.

Matthew Gale. Sworn the 27th day of May. 1824.

119

Evidence of Charles Motley

Mr. Charles Motley, Master of the ship Brothers, being Sworn, deposeth, that, on or about the 13th December last, there was a great deal of noise and disturbance amongst the women in the prison below; that he went down and found Mr. Hall in the act of dragging a woman through the prison gate; that the lights were out; that deponent endeavoured to get the woman out, but she was rescued from him, but who rescued her or aided so to do, he doth not know; that at this time Mr. Meach was in the prison and Mr. Hall was on the outside; that Lights were brought and deponent called for more assistance and proceeded into the Prison; that Mr. Hall pointed out the ringleaders and they were secured; that Cathrine McManus and Anne Russel, Lydia Gardner, Ellen Meadows, Cathrine Ryan and another woman were secured as the ringleaders and they were put down into the coal hole by orders of Mr. Hall. Saith that Mr. Hall complained that he had been very ill used in the prison and had been kicked and knocked down; thinks he saw a scratch on Mr. Hall's face the next morning, but will not say positively so; that the noise below continued for about 15 Minutes; Saith he was under no alarm for his own personal safety, but what it might have led to, if they had got the Doctor under their feet, or what the women might have done to him, they might have killed him. Saith that the gate of the prison opened on the outside, and no person inside could push against it without forcing it open. Saith that the reason he superseded Mr. Meach in December was in consequence of his having struck a woman prisoner on board, and not in reference to anything that took place on the night of the mutiny; that nothing had reached deponent suspicious of his conduct on that occasion. Saith that Mr. Meach always denied having anything to do with the women. Saith he heard Mr. Meach say he would shoot Mr. Hall when he got to Sydney, and went to his cabin and took out his pistols and examined the locks; saith he always had the highest opinion of him before. Saith that it was in the month of January and not in December that he superseded Mr. Meach. Saith that he was under no apprehensions for the safety of his ship on the voyage, as he had several respectable young men on board and his crew were to be confided in; Saith that he brought a light with him into the prison and it was there when he left the prison. Saith that Mr. Meach the next morning told deponent at breakfast that he had been throttled by the women, but no marks of violence appeared. Saith that the Light was in the prison and Mr. Gale was there, and Mr. Gale must have seen what

120

occurred in the prison by that light. Saith he was there about ten or twelve minutes and left the light there. Saith that Mr. Meach never refused his duty on board until he was superseded; believes, although Mr. Meach admitted he had taken Mary Smith out of the prison by means of false Keys, that he denied having had anything to do with the disturbance in the prison. Saith Mr. Meach had sailed with him before on a voyage to Jamaica, and behaved himself pretty well as Chief Mate. Saith on reference to his log book, it appears that Mr. Meach was suspended on the 15th of January and the disturbance took place on the 14th of December. Saith that he called for lights but they did not come until after the women had been secured.

Charles Motley.

Evidence of Lydia Gardner

Lydia Gardner, who came out a convict in the ship Brothers, being Sworn, deposeth, that, whilst the ship was at sea and the morning after Catherine Ryan had her hair cut off, she was on deck with Catherine McManus, Ellen Meadows, Elizabeth Reay and Ann Russel, Standing near the windlass. when Mr. Meach came up to them and said that the Boatswain had not behaved like a Man in letting Cathrine Ryan's hair being cut off and herself hand-cuffed, and that, if he Mr. Meach had had connexions with her, he would have lost his life sooner than her hair should have been cut off; and that it would serve the doctor right to give him a damned good milling; and that he Mr. Meach would give them a bottle of rum if they would do it, after it was over; and that he would come into the prison in a great hurry and appear to take Mr. Hall's part, but would take part with the women; that in the evening, when they were all locked down, there was a light in the prison which when it was inquired into, was instantly put out by Ann Russel, one of the convicts. The women then called out for Mr. Hall to bring another light; that Mr. Hall came down without a light and asked what was the matter: that no reply was made to him; that Mr. Hall called several times for Anne Russel to come out, but she would not go out; that Mr. Hall then came into the prison with a pair of handcuffs with which he struck Anne Russel several times; that a light was then brought from the hospital which was immediately knocked out: that they then made a great noise in the prison and Mr. Hall called for assistance and - Mr.

Meach Came down, followed by Captain Motley; that Mr. Meach came into the prison. Captain Motley remained in the hatchway; that Mr. Hall and Captain Motley had hold of Cathrine McManus's arm, trying to pull her out, When deponent and Anne Russel and Elizabeth Rae and Mr. Meach got hold of McManus trying to keep her in; that Mr. Meach had hold of her left Arm and told the Women not to let her go out; that they Succeeded in getting her away, and afterwards Mr. Meach desired Cathrine McManus to go to her bed and then Mr. Hall would not know who it was; that deponent then sat down by her berth to go to bed, and Mr. Hall took her out by force into the hatchway; did not see Mr. Gale in the Inside of the prison during the time, nor did she hear Mr. Gale have any conversation with Mr. Meach at this time; Saith that the same evening, whilst on deck, Mr. Meach came to deponent and said he would sooner lose his life than Mr. Hall should be hurt, and said this in the Captain's presence; and after the Captain was gone to his Cabin Mr. Meach told this deponent and some other women not to say anything that he was in it; Saith that she did not see Mr. Meach strike Mr. Hall, and Saith that, on the following Sunday Morning, Mr. Meach again desired the women not to let Mr. Hall get any thing out of them, as it would be settled in a few days. And Saith that deponent with four other women were on a chain some days afterwards, having been confined by order of Mr. Hall in consequence of the disturbance that had taken place, when Mr. Meach came up and expressed his sorrow that he could not do any thing for them but hoped they would not bring his name into question. Saith that deponent and the other women were confined in a dungeon for about six weeks by order of Mr. Hall, and for nine days had no bed to lie on, and three Weeks on bread and water; that they were chained together only one day for about two hours on the deck. Saith that Mr. Meach said he had heard that, if Mr. Hall had a pistol that night, he would have blown some of their brains out, but did not say whose brains, and Mr. Meach said that two could play at that. Saith that some time after, Thomas Robinson, a seaman on board, brought a message from Mr Meach to desire that when the women were brought to court to deny all they had said, and to say it was false; Saith that she cannot say that anything was done to Mr. Hall during the disturbance. Saith that from Mr. Hall's having struck Anne Russel with the handcuffs the blood followed, and the marks are now to be seen on her arm. Saith that the dungeon they were confined in was about 11 feet in length and 15 feet in breadth. Whilst the weather was very hot, and they were *nearly stifled for want of Air; that this was before they had crossed the Line. Saith that for the first four days they were closely confined in the dungeon, but afterwards some of them were allowed to be on deck for a few hours for four or five days. Saith that Sarah Twithridge, in deponent's presence, told Mr. Hall that she had heard Mr. Meach say he would give the women a bottle of rum; and Saith that she saw Mr. Meach strike Sarah Twithridge two or three times in the prison near her berth for having told Mr. Hall this.*

Evidence of Mr Richard Davis

Mr. Richard Davis, being Sworn, Deposeth, that he came out a passenger in the ship Brothers, and saith that, whilst the six women were in the dungeon in a state of confinement below at night, they gave him some statements to write in reference to the disturbance that had taken place on board amongst the women. That the women gave their statements in the hospital, and he and them read them in the cabin, and, when Elizabeth Reay had nearly finished her account, she was asked by Mr. Hall if she had any thing more to say, and then she said that Mr. Meach had assisted her with others in rescuing Cathrine McManus from the Captain and Mr. Hall; and this she said in the presence of this Deponent, Captain Motley and Mr. Hall. Saith that Mr. Hall, after the women had been confined in dungeon for about four Days, said to Deponent that he wished him to interfere to prevail with the other women on board to make intercession for the six Women in the dungeon to be released or their situation made more comfortable. Saith that Mr. Hall suggested this as a kind hearted man; and saith that the six women remained in the dungeon about a week without their bedding and on bread and water, during which they were brought out every day on deck. That Mr. Hall conducted himself more like a father to the female prisoners than otherwise; and Saith that this restraint upon the women was necessarily put on in order to enforce due subordination and submission on board. Saith he never saw the women chained together, but heard that they were once. That Ellen Meadows had on the Iron Collar for part of two Days. Saith that the morning after the disturbance a conversation took place with Deponent and Mr. Meach in reference to the disturbance, and Mr. Meach said he had been nearly throttled by one of the women, but doth not know that such a thing had happened. That Elizabeth Reay's statement was made in writing, which had been written by Mr.

Hall in her presence and the words taken down from her mouth; is not certain how long the women were in the dungeon, it be 9, 10, 11, or 12 Days. Some remained a longer time, and others, who were released, got in again for misconduct afterwards.

Richard. Davis. 24th June, 1824.

Dramatic scenes! Conflict and dispute! Accusations and enquiries aside, Elizabeth Reay was clearly directly involved in the so-called mutiny. I do find this surprising, if she was travelling with her baby.

The reason for the initial fracas also isn't very clear. It would appear that the Ship's Surgeon, James Hall, for whatever moral, ethical, religious or humanitarian purposes, had attempted to stop onboard prostitution. And this was the reward for his efforts. Whilst his intention was worthy, the reality was that prostitution onboard convict ships was generally a two-way arrangement, of mutual benefit. Crew and soldiers going to the colonies often wanted to satisfy their sexual needs. And some of the female prisoners (although certainly not all) wanted better food and conditions to see them through the voyage, or wanted to earn some money for their unknown futures. His worthy attempts to stop prostitution had earned James Hall enemies on both sides.

James Hall described the mutineers as:

Lydia Gardner - loose but quiet

Ellen Meadows - loose but quiet

Elizabeth Reay - disorderly and vicious

Catherine McManus - very loose and refractory

Ann Russell - an abandoned character.

Mary Smith - made her escape from the prison and slept with the first mate; very disobedient and guilty of mutiny.

I see that Elizabeth Reay is described as "disorderly and vicious," but not loose, which suggests the surgeon did not class her as a prostitute, but as a fighter – she may just have had a vicious tongue, rather than been physically vicious. The description "disorderly" usually referred to a woman of dubious morals – or a prostitute. This is also suggested by his description of most of the others as "loose" women. The fact that Elizabeth had got pregnant out of wedlock would account for such a description, anyway. At the time, chasteness until marriage was the ideal, and most still considered that women went into prostitution for either "lust or gain" rather than out of poverty or necessity.

Despite the comments on the female "mutineers" above, many of the women onboard *Brothers* seem to have been reasonably orderly and conducted themselves well. As we see from the statements, several of them had warned James Hall of the rebels' plans, in genuine concern for his life and welfare.

The Surgeon afterwards wrote in praise of the women convicts:

Port Jackson, May, 1824.

How steady is the pace of those who have forsaken the evil of their ways; such are the females (at least a great number) who have been under moral discipline in Newgate. I have every reason to be pleased with their exemplary conduct; they submit to restraint, and conform themselves to discipline.

The force of example and the value of moral discipline have been admirably shown in this voyage; and when I shall lay before you the proofs, you will become more sensible, perhaps, than you have been of the value of the labours in which you and your friends are employed, and may urge others to join in the same good work. A Missionary, who sailed in the same vessel, confirmed this pleasing statement. "For your comfort and encouragement, I beg leave to report to you the good conduct and decent behaviour of the Newgate women. That the kind instructions you have given them were not in vain, was very evident from their conduct during the voyage."

Elizabeth had arrived in Port Jackson.

The *Brothers* arrival indent describes her as follows:

Wray or Wreay, Elizabeth, Milkmaid & makes butter, tried at Penrith about 2 years ago. Sentence 7 years. Age, born 1805, [she was one of the youngest convicts onboard]. Height 5ft 3 1/2. Eyes Brown, Hair Dark brown, Complexion Brunet, Remarks - Mutinous Catholic.

However, the most interesting remark is written underneath:

Has one child, one year old, with her mother.

So, we now have the clarification that Elizabeth had, in fact, been pregnant at the time of her arrest; but the child had been left behind in England, with Elizabeth's mother.

Parramatta Female Factory

On arrival at the colony, female convicts were sent directly to the "Female Factory," where they learned to weave cloth. Some lived in at the factory and some were housed close by, going out to work at the factory daily. Many of the young, stronger girls only worked there for a few days before being assigned to other settlers to work as domestic servants.

It was very common for female convicts to marry very shortly after their arrival. Men outnumbered women at the colony by roughly 10 to 1, so they were very keen to marry, and the authorities encouraged this.

If a man wanted to make a new girl his wife, he simply applied to the factory, stating his intentions to choose one to marry.

The courtship process was very primitive and simple. The women would stand in a line and the man would walk up and down, appraising them by sight and making his choice. Once he had decided which of them he wanted, he would simply drop his handkerchief or scarf at the feet of his chosen woman. If she picked it up, it signified her consent to the proposal, and the marriage was undertaken very quickly, thereafter. At least the women had an element of choice. It wasn't a complete cattle-market after all, despite appearances.

Elizabeth was assigned to work as a servant for Mr Edward Charles Close, a settler and a churchman.

Born in 1790 in Bengal, India, Close had been educated in England. Entering the army in 1808, he served throughout the Peninsular War as a lieutenant in the 48th Regiment. On 3rd of August, 1817, he arrived in New South Wales with a detachment of his regiment onboard the *Matilda*. After spending several years in Sydney, he was transferred to Newcastle. As Acting Engineer in 1821-22, he was responsible for putting down mooring chains and removing dangerous shoals from Newcastle Harbour. He built a fort near the signal station and erected an iron beacon in which a large coal fire was lit each night at sunset. This light on Beacon Hill functioned until 1857, when it was replaced by the Nobby's Head light-house.

Exactly how long Elizabeth worked for Close is unclear. By the time of the 1826 muster, Elizabeth had been assigned as a servant to James Bardsley, a former convict who had arrived onboard the *Morley* in 1817. Does this ring the same bell for you, as it did for me? James Bardsley was married to Sarah Gregg, the daughter of James Gregg – Ann Gregg's brother.

Elizabeth Reay was the grand-daughter of Ann Gregg's other brother, John. So, Elizabeth had been placed as a servant to her own mother's cousin. That can't have been a coincidence. This work assignment must have been purposefully arranged, since there was that family connection. Freed convicts often sought reunions with convict family members by putting in a request that the convict relative be assigned to work for them. Families tried to look after their own.

I discovered that Elizabeth Reay married William Grose at St John' Church, Parramatta, on 18th September, 1826.

The 1828 census shows William and Elizabeth Grose living together with two children Martha Ray, age 3, and William Grose, aged 8 months. So, Elizabeth must have had an illegitimate daughter before marrying.

Her husband William's occupation is shown on the census as a "shoe maker". This seems ironic, since Elizabeth had been transported for stealing a pair of shoes. Hopefully, he kept her in shoes for life.

Chapter 18
1822 - Ann Irving

I mentioned earlier that the first time I found Ann Irving engaging in criminal activity was in 1822, according to a report on the county's quarter sessions.

Cumberland Paquet April 22nd 1822

Ann Irvin and Isabella Cuthbertson were put to the bar, charged with stealing a lead cistern, in the parish of Camerton, on the 5th March last, the property of Isabella Craig.

Mr Courtney, for the prosecution, said Isabella Craig resided at Seaton. On the night of the 5th March, a very stormy one, and therefore fit for depredation, the cistern was stolen, and the evidence would show why the prisoners were charged with theft.

Isabella Craig, sworn - I am a single woman residing at Seaton in the parish of Camerton, and the prisoners live about a quarter mile off. On the 5th March I had a leaden cistern in my yard; the night was very stormy; on the next morning it had disappeared. I traced footsteps to the house of Irving, where I saw a dross of lead, and such appearances as indicated that a large fire had been lighted in the middle of the floor. The men named Hutchinson and Irving were in the house, but neither of the prisoners. Wm. Baty soon afterwards set out in search of them.

Wm Baty - I went with Miss Craig to Irvings house, where I saw the appearance of a fire and the dross of lead. I found two saws there (he produced them) on which are blue marks as if used in cutting lead. I went off to Whitehaven in quest of the prisoners, and overtook Geo Irving on the road (who was before in the house), by which my suspicions were excited, and I gave him in custody to another man, and went onwards.

Arrived at Whitehaven, I met the prisoners just coming out of the town with a horse and cart. I charged them with stealing lead; they said they knew nought about anything of the kind, they had been selling besoms. I searched the cart and found several small pieces of lead, and there were blue marks as if lead had been carried in it. I applied to Nicholson, the constable, who asked them to whom they had sold the lead, and they again denied having had any.

The prisoners were afterwards taken to Mr Gordon's shop, and there Irving acknowledged she had sold lead to him, observing she might do what she liked with her own. I said, "It is the stolen lead melted up." She replied, "We must do some way; you almost hungered us last winter." I don't know that she at times dealt in old iron.

Thomas Gordon, sworn - I am a brazier in Whitehaven. On the 7th of March last year, Cuthbertson came to me and asked what I gave for old lead. I told her the price, she went out, and immediately both the prisoners came with a cart and horse, and brought a cake of melted lead with them, which was in a rough state, and appeared to have been hastily cooled. They afterwards brought more, and seeing so large a quantity, I wished to know how they came by it. Irving said it had been a whole winter's work for them to collect it - ever since Martinmas. I bought the lead, 352 lbs, and paid £2 4s 0d for it.

Whitehaven is nine miles from their home in Seaton: a fair distance on horse and cart. Despite their claim that they were selling brooms, it wasn't even a market day at Whitehaven, so there was no excuse to go there, except to sell the lead. The nearest town, Workington, is only one mile away from Seaton and there were plumbers there, where they could have sold the lead far more quickly and easily. Why would they go all the way to Whitehaven? If this was genuinely their own lead, it would make more sense to go to the nearest town to sell it. Was it too close to home, and were they too well known in Workington?

This was the case for the prosecution:

Mr Aglionby submitted to the bench that there was nothing to go to the Jury. The case, as opened, was one of possession. There was no evidence of identity of property.

The prisoners having been asked if they had anything to offer in their defence,

*Irving said that when Baty first came up to her, he **** her for a ****, and said he would banish her out of the parish. She had a large family and they wanted to get rid of her. A fire could not have been lighted in the middle of the house in the night, the smoke would have suffocated the children. There had been much rain, the floor was wet, and she had strewn ashes over it to keep down the water.*

Cuthbertson said she knew nothing about the lead; she met Irving in Whitehaven.

The chairman shortly summed things up, and the Jury immediately found the prisoners Not Guilty.

The circumstantial evidence from the witnesses would suggest her guilt, but as she said, her neighbours wanted to get rid of her, and could have been lying.

Well, in the end, the jury found her not guilty primarily because there was no evidence to prove the identity of the owner of the lead.

But – was she really guilty? I'll leave you to make your own mind up.

The thing I found difficult to understand was why Ann used her maiden name of Irving, and not her married name: Hutchinson. Could this be just a typical ruse, common of criminals at that time, in an attempt to disguise her true identity?

Chapter 19
1824 - The Hutchinson Family

I was now squarely focused on the Hutchinson's, hoping to find more evidence of criminal activity. It didn't take long.

Searching the England and Wales criminal registers 1791 – 1892, just using "William Hutchinson" and "Cumberland" as my search criteria, I simply couldn't believe my eyes. Here they were, again.

The 1824 epiphany assizes featured the three siblings: George, Jane, and Mary Hutchinson as being convicted of larceny, and William Hutchinson and Ann Irvin, their parents, being convicted for receiving stolen goods. The whole family were sentenced to seven years' transportation. You just couldn't make this lot up, if you tried!

I went straight to the British Newspaper Archives, making a basic search for "Hutchinson" and "1824", and there I found the whole story.

The Carlisle Patriot reported on the County assizes, held at Cockermouth, on the 17th of January 1824.

Carlisle Patriot 17th January 1824

William Hutchinson, Ann Irving, George Hutchinson, Jane Hutchinson, Mary Hutchinson and John Allen, were indicted for stealing on the 22nd of October last, in the Parish of Great Broughton, 17 tame and reclaimed geese, value 17s, the property of Messrs. Whittaker. Another count charged two of the prisoners with stealing, and the others with receiving the geese, knowing them to be stolen. All pleaded not guilty.

Mr. Courtney appeared for the prosecutors. He said the circumstances of the case were so clear as to leave no doubt of bringing the offence home to the prisoners. Three of the Hutchinson's were the grown-up children of Hutchinson and Allen, [a clear error: it should be "Irving"] who lived together as man and wife, but were not so in reality.

Geo. Whittaker sworn – Witness, was a good looking strong young man, but the court, council and Jury had infinite trouble in making him speak up so as to be heard, small as the place is. - On 22nd of October (he said) I and my brother had a flock of geese in partnership; I myself had others, my personal property. On that day, the whole were together in a stubble field. On the 23rd, 17 of them had disappeared. We attempted to trace them. There were marks on the ground of a pair of strong shoes, caulkered at the heel; also of a pair of sharp nibbed clogs; and likewise of two odd clogs worn by a person, the toe of one of which was sharp, the other round, with a caulker off the right heel. We traced the steps towards Seaton, and saw three people at a distance, who ran away. A warrant was obtained, and we went with it to Seaton, where the prisoners resided, and reached Hutchinson's house about twelve at night. A great smoke issued from the chimney: the family were up, and appeared to be very busy, and there was a strong smell of burning feathers. We stopped outside till a quarter before seven in the morning; they were busy until about three o'clock. We went in and found the bodies of thirteen geese lately plucked, quite warm. They were upstairs beside an old chimney; a square box was set in front, and they were covered with hay. We also found twenty six wings under an old bed, carefully concealed. There are only two rooms in the house. There were some young children in bed; but the prisoners were all up, and covered with down. Three feet and four wings were found, which I knew from certain marks. The shoes and clogs of George, Jane and Mary precisely corresponded with the marks in the field.

Cross-examined by Mr. Aglionby for the prisoners. - I saw the marks of the feet in the stubble field, where the geese had been driven into a corner and caught; also in two adjoining fields lately laid down; there is an occupation road within one hundred yards of the field. I live in Broughton, I don't know if Mary [should be Ann] Irving is Hutchinson's wife or not. I took up the father, mother and children down to nine years old, and a lodger. The elder prisoner works at the collieries as a basket-maker. John Allen is a tinker; he said he was only a lodger. The house contains but two rooms, one above another, very small rooms; there was no down flying about from the beds, for they slept upon straw. I did not take the shoes and clogs and compare them with the marks in the fields. Clogs and caulkers are worn by many persons in this neighbourhood. The wings were cut off when found, and had not been pulled. (Three wings produced) I can swear to them by the colour; I have no other mark to go by. (Three feet produced) These I myself marked in the web, and never saw any others marked like them.

- The cross-examination was extended to a great length, and on the whole, was strongly confirmatory of the evidence in chief.

By Mr. Courtney - One of the caulkers was wanting on the right heel of the clog of one of the prisoners. There was not much accommodation for lodgers in the house. The geese with the marked feet were mine. Two were so marked; and I found three feet and four wings; I can't speak as to the others.

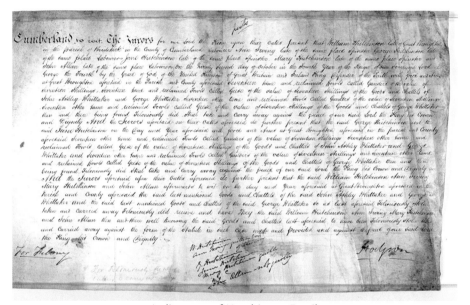

Indictment of Hutchinson Family

Thos.' Harding. constable, was present at the search, cross-examined - He did not know that Irving was married to Hutchinson. Never saw Allen there before.

John Ismay, constable, had heard all Mr. Whittaker had said - It was perfectly correct.

John Bowman swore – I am a neighbour of the prisoners. I have seen Allen several times with the family.

Cross examined - I cannot say that they keep a lodging house. I heard a man once comment that he had applied for lodgings there, and that they would take him in.

No witness was called to character, nor was any proof of marriage offered. Mr, Aglionby privately communicated with the elder prisoners before the case went to the Jury, but he apparently could illicit nothing from them of favourable nature.

The chairman summed up the evidence. With respect to the prisoner Allen, he observed there was no proof to criminate him.

The Jury having consulted some minutes returned the following verdict. - George, Jane, Mary Hutchinson, Guilty generally; that is guilty of stealing; Wm. Hutchinson and Ann Irving, Guilty of receiving; John Allen, not Guilty.

Chairman - a perfectly proper verdict, according to the evidence.

The convicted five was sentenced to be transported for a period of seven years. They are a notorious family.

I found it interesting that, during the court case, they seemed to make a thing of whether or not William and Ann were married. The baptism documents of all three of the children who had been convicted with them clearly stated "Ann, wife of William Hutchinson, late Irvin". Would they lie in church? As poor as they were, they would have feared Gods wrath and I doubted they would lie.

Cockermouth Moot Hall

The Hutchinson's were tried at the County assizes, held in Cockermouth. In 1824, the Court Leet, or Manor Court, was held upstairs in the Moot Hall, located in the market place. The Moot Hall building was later demolished in 1829 and its stone used to build the new Court House next to the River Cocker, which still stands today.

From their arrest until they appeared in court, the family were held in the Cockermouth House of Correction, opposite the Bowling Green Inn on St Helen's Street. The House of Correction was known locally as "Billy Mackreth's Parlour," named after the gaol-house keeper William Mackreth, whose reputation was one of ruthlessness. After the trial, they were sent to the County Gaol in Carlisle, while arrangements were made for their transportation. A warrant for removal of the prisoners was issued on September 6th.

The next newspaper article I found read:

Lancashire Gazette 2nd October 1824

The following convicts were sent off from Carlisle gaol for the hulks at Woolwich, on Wednesday week; - Charles Samuel Cave (of Thornley Abbey, Cambridgeshire, Esq. and so forth!) John Taylor, William Hutchinson, George Hutchinson, Peter Holmes and John Smith. The old gaol is well rid of such troublesome customers.

Searching the prison hulk registers, I eventually found a document from the *Justitia* moored at Woolwich, showing "Prisoner 7965 Hutchinson, Geo." The gaoler's report said, "bad character" and "How disposed of: NSW".

Then, sadly, "Prisoner 7964 Hutchinson Will'm. Gaolers report, bad character. How disposed of: Dead."

William hadn't made it. Further searches of the *Justitia*'s registers brought up another document showing that William had died on 29th November, 1825, just a little over a year after being sent from Carlisle to the hulks at Woolwich.

The *Justitia* was a 260-ton prison hulk, originally built in 1777. She had been moored in the Thames when the American War of Independence put a stop to the transportation of criminals to the former colonies. The *Justitia* belonged to the shipowner, Duncan Campbell, who was the government contractor who organised the prison-hulk system at that time. Campbell was involved in the shipping of convicts to the penal colony at Botany Bay (in fact, to Port Jackson, just to the north of present-day Sydney) in New South Wales; with the first fleet going out in 1788.

The reputation of the hulks was so bad that many convicts preferred to be hanged rather than to go onboard them. Convicts were often admitted to the ships suffering from a complete depression of their spirits, made all the worse by having usually been put to hard physical labour in full view of the public.

Politicians at the time were becoming concerned about the corruption of morals in a system that kept hardened criminals, first offenders and young boys all together in one confined space. Children as young as eight appear on hulk registers. Prisoners slept, ate and passed all non-working time in the same crowded space, below deck. Sleeping arrangements were cramped and airless, providing ideal conditions for the spread of disease, including typhus and tuberculosis. Death rates were high, especially in the early years, when roughly one in four inmates died on the hulks.

Sadly, William was too old and not strong enough to withstand these vile conditions for longer than a year, and at the age of 72, he died. So many prisoners died on the hulks that they were buried in unmarked mass graves, somewhere in the Woolwich arsenal. And presumably, William lies there, too.

His son, George, had also been on board the hulk *Justitia*; but after looking into convict records, I discovered that he had been transported along with one hundred and twenty other prisoners onboard the *Minstrel*, which set sail on the 5th of April, 1825, under the command of Charles Arkoll. George had been transported almost eight months before his father had died. This suggests that old William must have been deemed completely unfit for the journey, probably suffering from severe illness for a considerable time before his death.

From Woolwich, the *Minstrel* first went upriver, where the guard – which consisted of the 57th regiment under the orders of Lieutenant Shadforth – embarked. She left London on the 10th April for Portsmouth, departing from there on the 17th April in the company of the *Norfolk*.

All prisoners on board arrived in Port Jackson in good health, although it was reported that there had been an outbreak of scurvy in about twenty of the men, early in July. Hugh Walker, the Ship's Surgeon Superintendent, kept a medical journal from 19th March to 26 August, 1825. The journal, which is in the National Archives, contains details of the medical treatment of those put on the sick list. There is no mention of George there, so he must have had a relatively healthy and uneventful journey.

The *Minstrel* arrived in Port Jackson on 22nd August, 1825. Three days later, on 25th August, the order was given that boats were to be placed alongside the *Minstrel* the following morning, to disembark the prisoners. The Sydney

View of the JUSTITIA HULK, with the Convicts at Work, near Woolwich.

The Justitia

Gazette reported that the prisoners had been landed, and underwent the usual inspection in the prison-yard by Lieutenant Governor Stewart, who addressed the men in the usual way.

After the convicts had been formally handed over into the charge of the Governor, the prisoners were often segregated, with the most hardened criminals being sent to special prisons or areas. The rest acted as servants to the settlers, or carried out hard labour, in gangs.

By day, the prisoners were supervised by a military guard and convict overseers, and at night, they were locked up in small wooden huts behind stockades.

Convict discipline was harsh. For those convicts who committed further offences in the colony, punishments were brutal. There was the cat o' nine tails – a whip divided into nine thongs with knots in them designed to lacerate victims' skin so it bled and caused extreme pain. Fifty lashes were a common punishment – unimaginable in its cruelty. Equally feared was serving time on the chain gangs, where convicts were shackled together in ankle irons or chains weighing ten pounds or more and employed in the back-breaking work of making new roads. This was hard labour, with extra pain and discomfort.

Most convicts were assigned to work for settlers and freed convicts who had lodged an application for a convict servant or worker with the Governor. The authorities were not completely heartless, well-behaved convicts could make an application or petition the Governor to have their families brought out from England to join them. Although that wasn't a totally altruistic act on the authorities' behalf, since it also helped to populate and establish the colony. In some cases, convict servants and workers could be assigned to work for their free settler families – as seemed to be the case for Elizabeth Reay (Ann Gregg's great-niece).

The next information I found about George Hutchinson is in the Australian 1828 census, where he is recorded as employed by James Evans and his wife, Isabella Evans, nee Irving (ding, bells ringing again); both freed convicts. I made a note of that name "Irving" to explore any possible connections to Ann Irving, later.

Conduct registers were kept to monitor behaviour and convicts who worked hard and caused no trouble could obtain their "ticket of leave", even before their sentence expired or they were pardoned. This "ticket", was a document given to convicts that granted them freedom to work and live within a given district of the colony. There were other conditions attached. Under a ticket of leave, church attendance and appearance before a magistrate were compulsory. However, there was a bonus: convicts granted a ticket of leave were allowed to own property.

There were two kinds of pardons available, which effectively freed convicts. Conditional pardons were granted on condition that convicts did not return to England or Ireland. Absolute pardons allowed convicts to return to England, since their sentences were totally cleared. However, due to the high cost of the journey, very few did return.

George Hutchinson received his certificate of freedom on 10th of May, 1831. The following year, 1832, on 27th of February, he married Eleanor Maxwell at St John's Church, Parramatta, New South Wales. George and Eleanor produced eleven children, of which ten survived. They bought 40 acres of land in 1850, and George worked as a harness maker and farmer. He died on 28th August 1878 and went to his final resting place at Mutton Falls cemetery, Tarans, N.S.W

Ann Irvin/Irving – who became Ann Hutchinson, caused me a lot of confusion, since her name is spelled both ways. Most of the population at this time were illiterate, and simply didn't know how to spell their own names. Neither did the people of authority they spoke to, or those who recorded those names. Therefore, the name's spelling could vary considerably, depending on how the writer heard it, or decided to spell it. The fact that people had regional accents or dialects, as they had in the Borders, made the problem worse.

I've said that the baptismal records for George, Mary and Jane all gave their mother's name as Ann "Hutchinson late Irvin", which suggests that she was married to William. However, as I previously mentioned, in the court case and newspaper reports, it seemed that the Court, for some reason, wanted to expose Ann as not being married to William. I wasn't sure what to make of this. If William and Ann were not married, their children would have been recorded on their baptismal documents as "bastard children",this was a perfectly normal term, used for illegitimate children at that time. The children hadn't been given that label, making it all the more likely that William and Ann were married.

It was proving impossible to find evidence of their marriage. Before the introduction of the Civil Registration Act of 1836, which came into effect on July 1st 1837, there were no marriage certificates as we know them today. If the couple were married in church, it was recorded in parish registers. The vast majority of the population were deeply religious, making church marriages almost mandatory. Normally, to prove a marriage, the couple could get a letter from the parish clergyman or anyone else of authority in the parish where they had settlement, or had been married. This was enough proof of marriage.

Presumably they didn't have anything like that available to show in court. Perhaps the reason William and Ann couldn't prove their marriage was because they had been married in a parish in another area.

Ann was lucky – rather than being transported, she had her sentence commuted, and her time was to be served in Carlisle goal. This leniency was recorded as due to her "great age". At the time of the crime, Ann was approximately 60. The government much preferred to transport younger, fertile women; since they saw the transportation of female prisoners of marriageable age as a way to populate the colonies. They believed that having wives and family would have a calming effect on the male convicts. There was a huge imbalance in the ratio of men to women in the penal colonies, which caused unrest. It was thought that this brooding, violent atmosphere could be quelled by increasing the female population.

So, females were sent to the colonies primarily for breeding purposes. Ann was clearly too old for this, so her age saved her from transportation.

After serving less than five of her seven-year sentence in Carlisle gaol, on 29th July 1828, an application was made for her pardon. The application was sent to the Home Secretary at that time: Robert Peel, founder of the modern police force.

The appeal stated that Ann's conduct had been exemplary and her habits industrious. Two days later, on 31st July, 1828, Ann was granted a free pardon and released.

She could now live her old age in peaceful retirement.

Except for the fact that, only one year later, Ann was in trouble again.

Carlisle Patriot 13th June 1829

Ann Irving, committed by John Hodgson Esq., for stealing from the shop of Mr Jos. Railton, mercer of Carlisle, eleven yards of printed cloth, of the value 10s

This seemed to be a crime more fitting to Ann Gregg and her gang! My searches of prison records revealed that she was sentenced to six months in Carlisle gaol.

All seemed quiet for a decade. At least, as far as I could find. Goodness knows whether she became a model citizen, somehow I doubted it.

However, ten years later, and now using the name of Ann (Nanny) Hutchinson, she was convicted with Charles and Christiana Berry (her daughter Mary Ann's in-laws) for "uttering base coin" – that is, circulating counterfeit money.

140

Sir

(Carlisle 29th July 1840?)

The visiting Magistrates of the Gaol of this County, having certified to the last General Quarter Sessions of the Peace, holden at Carlisle on the 15 day of July Instant, that Ann Irving who was convicted of Larceny at the Epiphany Quarter Sessions 1834 and sentenced to be transported for 7 years, was a fit object for the Recommendation of the Court to the Mercy of the Crown; her said Sentence not having been carried into Execution in consequence of her great Age: and that she had ever since her Conviction remained a Prisoner in the said Gaol, under the said Sentence, where her Conduct had been exemplary, and her habits industrious. I am therefore directed by the said Court of Quarter Sessions to apply for his Majesty's most gracious pardon for the said Ann Irving——

I have the Honor to be
Your most obedient
humble Servant

To the Rt. Honble.
Robert Peel &.

W. Hodgson

Ann Irving's Plea for Clemency

She was sentenced on August 13th, 1839, to one year's imprisonment – with hard labour. That must have been tough for a very old woman. Hopefully, she just had to pick oakum rather than the more strenuous physical tasks that punishment entailed. Her release would have been in or around July 1840.

141

Ann Irving
Free Pardon George R

Whereas Ann Irving was at the Epiphany Quarter Session of the Peace 1824, holden for the County of Cumberland tried and convicted of Larceny and Sentenced to be Transported Seven Years for the same; We in consideration of some circumstances humbly represented unto Us, are Graciously Pleased to Extend Our Grace and Mercy unto her, and to Grant her Our Free Pardon for the Crime of which she stands Convicted Our Will and Pleasure therefore is that you cause her the said

Ann

Ann Irving's Free Pardon

Millbank Penitentiary

Chapter 20
1824 - The Hutchinson Girls

I'd traced the fates of William and George Hutchinson, as well as Ann Irving. What happened to the other goose-thieves, Jane and Mary Ann? To find out, I had to go back to local newspapers.

Like the others, William and Ann's daughters, Jane and Mary Ann, were also held in Carlisle goal.. Their letter of removal was signed on the 9th of November, 1824. Shortly afterwards, they were sent to London for transportation.

Cumberland Paquet 7th December 1824

Eight persons, under sentence of transportation, were last week removed from Carlisle gaol; viz. William Chatterton, William Strong, James Davidson, Arthur Kelly, Edward Dobson, and John Surgeon, for the hulks at Woolwich; Mary Hutchinson, and Jane Hutchinson, for the Penitentiary at Millbank.

Designed by the architect Robert Smirke, Millbank Penitentiary opened in 1816. It cost half a million pounds to build and was the largest prison in England. Only eight years later, the teenaged Hutchinson sisters were confined there, and for all its relative newness, it still wasn't a pleasant environment. An interesting description was given in the Penny Illustrated several decades later.

Penny Illustrated Paper 19th October 1865

If the ground-plan of the building at Millbank is a geometrical puzzle, the interior is assuredly an eccentric maze. Long, dark and narrow corridors and twisting passages, in which the visitor unaccustomed to the dubious twilight has to feel his way; double-locked doors opening at all sorts of queer angles, and leading sometimes into blind entries and frequently to the stone staircases... so steep and narrow, are not unlike the devious steps by which the traveller reaches the towers of Strasbourg and some other cathedrals, except that they are even more gloomy.

Females sentenced to transportation were seldom held on prison hulks, but were instead held at Newgate Prison or Millbank Penitentiary. Conditions at even the relatively modern Millbank prison were atrocious, with minimal basic rations of bread and water. Even worse were the dreadful sanitary conditions causing regular outbreaks of cholera, dysentery and scurvy. These appalling conditions were reported in 1823.

Morning Chronicle 14th July 1823

The two chief sources of disease incident to man are marsh-miasmata and human effluvia. In the Penitentiary these sources are not only combined but concentrated. It is seated in a marsh, beneath the bed of the river, through which the vapours from stagnant water are constantly exhaling. The effluvia from the mass of human beings confined within its walls cannot dissipate from deficient ventilation.

These causes operating upon a crown of persons, whose minds are depressed by the prospect of lingering confinement, cannot fail to produce all the disease which take place in the Lazar-house: scrophula, scurvy, prostration of strength, and fever of the worse description. To these sources of disease must be added the malaria from the muddy banks of the river, which renders the whole vicinity unhealthy... There is but one remedy - to place as much gun powder under the foundation as may suffice to blow the whole fabric into the air. Whether it would be an act of humanity, previously to the removal of the prisoners, may be a fit subject for discussion by those sapient persons who first sanctioned the erection of such a structure on such a site.

Only eight years after it was built, and just one year after this damning report, young Jane and Mary Ann Hutchinson were incarcerated there. To say that it makes my skin crawl is an understatement.

It would be so easy to launch into a diatribe about the inhumanity of the system, but who am I to judge? It's just how it was at that time in our history, when human life was cheap. Nothing can change the past; but thank goodness we have learned from it.

Jane and Mary Ann must have been looking forward to the voyage, just to get away from this dreadful place, but apparently, their circumstances changed.

An undated Millbank Penitentiary register tells us a little bit about the girls:

Mary Hutchinson, Seaton, Cumberland, age 16, worked in the fields, single, no children, 5ft tall, sandy hair, fair complexion, blue eyes. Mark from a cut on her forehead and another on the left side of her left eye.

Jane Hutchinson, Seaton, Cumberland, age 19, worked in the fields, single, no children, 4ft 9 3/4in tall, brown hair, fair complexion, grey eyes. Mark from a cut under lip.

Both girls have an "expiration of sentence" date of 14th April, 1829. That meant they would only serve five years of their seven-year sentence. I can only assume this was dependent on good behaviour.

I have no idea what happened during the years which followed, until the next document I found, which was a petition for a pardon. And, they were still in Millbank. Somehow these two young girls had avoided transportation.

The petition says:

Both of these female prisoners have been remarkably well conducted young women ever since they came into the Penitentiary. They appear to have been very unfortunate in their parents, who are both Convicts - They have a brother, a Blacksmith residing at Dearham near Wigton in Cumberland, who will receive them until they can procure situations. - They have been always employed in the Laundry, and have made themselves very useful. They are well able to earn their living.

So, that was the end of that. On April 14th, 1829, the girls were released.

The interesting point in the petition (seen on the next page) is the remark that they were to be released into the care of their brother, a blacksmith. So far as I could see, William and Ann only had three children, and their brother George was in Australia. Could Ann have had another family before she met William?

We know that William did – with his first wife, Ann Gregg – so it's quite possible that this blacksmith was a half-brother from a previous marriage.

Shortly after their release, Mary Ann went on to marry – as I discovered later.

Jane simply disappears. I don't think it was a case of cloaks and daggers disappearing. Jane probably married after her release. In doing this, her surname would change, making her very difficult to find.

These six prisoners have uniformly behaved themselves well; and the whole have friends to receive them, upon their being discharged.

Mary Hutchinson & Jane Hutchinson Sisters, both tried for the same Offence. Convicted at Cockermouth 13th Jany 1824 – Received here 6th Decemr following. their time expires 14th April 1829 –

Both of these female Prisoners have been remarkably well conducted Young Women ever since they came into the Penitentiary; they appear to have been very unfortunate in their Parents, who are both Convicts? – They have a brother a blacksmith, residing at Dearham near Wigton in Cumberland, who will receive them until they can procure situations. – They have been always employed in the Laundry; and have made themselves very useful – they are well able to earn their living. –

Hannah Besford, – Convicted at Shrewsbury 16th July 1824 – Received here 6th July 1825. – Her time expires 25th Oct. 1829.

This

Jane and Ann's petition for clemency
146

Chapter 21
1828 - Isabella Irving

As I previously mentioned, the Australian 1828 census shows Ann Hutchinson late Irvin's son, George Hutchinson, working as a labourer and living with James Evans and his wife, Isabella Evans, nee Irving – both ex-convicts. The name Irving had jumped out at me. Could there be a connection between Ann Irvin and Isabella Irving? Or was this just a coincidence?

James Evans had arrived in 1820 on the convict ship Asia 2, Isabella arrived on the *Janus* the same year.

Australian records for transported convicts are pretty comprehensive. Once you've worked out which documents hold relevant information, it's reasonably easy to follow them from gaol in England, through to the penal colonies. In this case, my starting point was in Australia, so I had to research all of this in reverse.

I'd already explored all the different types of convict documents, so I knew what to look for. I knew from the census that the ship that Isabella had been transported on was the *Janus*, so I had a reasonable starting point.

The *Janus* landed at New South Wales on 5th May 1820, with Isabella onboard. The ship had sailed from England on 23rd October, 1819, carrying one hundred and five female prisoners, twenty six children and several passengers, including Reverend Philip Connelly and Reverend John Joseph Therry. The ship stopped at the Cove of Cork, Ireland, where another forty-four female prisoners embarked. Then, the *Janus* left Ireland on 5th December, 1819, bound for New South Wales, calling at Rio de Janeiro en route, to collect provisions.

Of the 104 convicts onboard, one died on the voyage, as did the ship's surgeon. On arrival, the Captain, Thomas Mowat, was criticised by Lieutenant Governor Macquarie for not putting in to port for assistance, particularly since James Creagh, the surgeon, was one of the casualties.

After arrival in the colony, it was customary for convicts to be questioned about their treatment during the voyage, and all who were asked reported that they had been looked after very well.

However, within a couple of weeks of their arrival, Governor Macquarie was advised that perhaps things had not gone all that well during the voyage.

Mr Nicholas Bayly, a free settler, informed Macquarie by letter that two of the Janus women who had been assigned to him as servants were pregnant. One, Mary Long, claimed that it was Mowat, the Captain, who was responsible for her condition. The other, Lydia Esden, revealed that the man responsible for her pregnancy was John Hedges, Mowat's chief mate. Mr. Bayly told Macquarie that the women had freely admitted that they had lived in a state of prostitution with the men throughout the voyage.

In response, Macquarie asked the Bench of Magistrates in Sydney to investigate the matter immediately and to report back to him. Within a week, the Bench met to hear testimony from those allegedly involved, and other key witnesses.

The proceedings show that the first person to be interviewed was Mrs Ann Moore, the wife of Corporal Moore of the 48th Regiment. Although she had come out onboard Janus as a passenger, she had chosen to share the prison room with the convicts in preference to taking a berth in the sick bay, which was the only other accommodation available. As such, she had been in a good position to observe the behaviour of the prisoners and the conduct of the captain and crew towards them. Whilst she admitted that it was impossible to see the captain's cabin from her berth, she was certain that no female convict was ever there for any length of time and that those who did enter that cabin did so briefly, and only for the purpose of obtaining Mowat's linen to wash and mend, and return it afterwards. She added that the prisoners were invariably ordered below decks every evening, that the hatches were then securely fastened, and that the sailors were never down with the women at night. Mrs Moore told the Bench that the prisoners had been admonished from time to time for riotous conduct and swearing but that this conduct had amounted only to fighting among themselves and card-playing. She had even seen some of them tipsy occasionally. But she had not seen any of the sailors coming into the prison room except when they had legitimate business there. She thought that the captain and his officers were kind and that they did everything they could to make the prisoners and everybody on board comfortable. She added that she was aware that two sailors had been put off the vessel before it had left Cork for speaking to the women and that during the voyage the captain had frequently rebuked the seamen when he saw them speaking to the prisoners.

148

Father Connolly, the senior of the priests, was the next to be interviewed. He told the Bench that from his first day aboard Janus he had had reason to suspect that some kind of improper intercourse was going on between the female convicts and the sailors. He had observed women coming from the sailors' berth and believed that it was common for the men to take a partner from the prison room. He was aware that two or three women were often, indeed constantly, in the captain's cabin. He had overheard Captain Mowat and Surgeon Creagh openly discussing this matter and, at the beginning, he had raised the matter frequently with the captain. Later, however, he had ceased to do so because he was convinced that doing so was useless. At Rio, Connolly said, a letter had been sent to Commodore Bowles who was in charge there to alert him to malpractices on board. As a consequence of this, Mowat and Creagh had gone ashore to arrange for more bolts and bars to be brought aboard to keep the prison secure, and to prevent prostitution. The new bolts were soon removed, and the hatches broken open as regularly as they were fastened down. After Rio, prostitution seemed to prevail more than before and, to a most shameful extent. Connolly believed that while Mowat seemed, by his words, to want to stop what was happening, his actions spoke otherwise. He was setting such a bad example that the seamen, who seemed determined to have the women, were actually encouraged to continue in what they were doing. On the other hand, he believed that Creagh had done everything he could to prevent what was occurring.

But Connolly was adamant that the entire blame for this conduct could not be laid at the feet of the captain and crew. The women, he asserted, were as determined to communicate with the sailors as they themselves were with the women. Connelly said that when Creagh attempted to punish the women for this he was only laughed at. He was not supported by the captain and officers in the performance of his duty, and he had had no assistance from any quarter. When, after leaving Rio, Creagh told Mowat that if he could not have his support then he himself must accept full responsibility for the prisoners, there was an altercation between them.

Next to be heard by the Bench of Magistrates was Father Therry. Like Connolly, he said that he had quickly become aware of the utmost prevalence of vice aboard Janus. In his view, what was happening on the ship amounted to general criminal intercourse between the sailors and the convicts. It was general and widespread.

In Therry's opinion, the locks and bars that had been taken on at Rio were of poor quality and easily opened with any key. Some of the locks had been thrown overboard. A number of the boards which separated the men's berths from the women's had large gaps between them and this facilitated easy communication between them. He added that, to his knowledge, the Catholic prisoners, that is the Irish women, who comprised about one third of the total, had not entered into the illicit intercourse between the sexes. He concluded his testimony by stating his conviction that if a proper system of discipline had been established by the captain early in the voyage, none of the illicit intercourse would have prevailed.

Captain Mowat was then called before the Bench. Strenuously denying that any irregularity had occurred aboard the vessel during its voyage, he asserted that the evidence against him and his crew would soon be shown to be vague and inconclusive.

Mowat unequivocally denied the accusation that he had had a female named Mary Long as a constant companion in his cabin. He stressed that it was only because she washed for him during the voyage that she entered his cabin and, in doing so, had done no more than other prisoners, namely, Mary Hoare, Isabella Irvin, and Ellen Molloy who performed the same service for the surgeon and the priests.

Convict Mary Long was then called to the Bench. In a sworn statement, she said that when first put aboard Janus, she had been placed in the prison room and that it was locked down after dark. At daylight, the hatches were unlocked and the prisoners were able to come up on deck. After sailing from Cork, however, the prisoners were not mustered again and, while she was not aware of any woman being taken out of the prison room after lock down time in the evening, she was unable to say whether all of them were actually in the prison room when the lock down took place. In her own case, she said, while she did not frequently spend the night in Captain Mowat's cabin, she was there when not in the prison room at night. As a result, she was now in her present pregnant condition – and, for this, she said the captain was responsible. She told the Bench that she knew that Lydia Esden had spent nights in the cabin of the Chief Mate, Mr Hedges. She was unable to say whether other women were down in the sailors' berths but she believed they were, and that this situation continued 'days and nights'. The women, she said, had been treated very well by the sailors and had no complaints about what was happening. She had heard the surgeon complain of the women's 'disorderly' behaviour, but he had urged them to keep what was happening from the priests. He told the women that 'he knew what he was doing'.

Lydia Esden was then sworn in. She stated that shortly after arrival in Sydney she had been assigned as a servant to Mr Nicholas Bayly, to whom she had written complaining that she was pregnant to Mr Hedges. She had explained to Bayly that she was aware that Janus, with Hedges aboard, was about to leave Sydney on a whaling expedition and that it was urgent that she be permitted to go into Sydney to speak to him about monetary support. She told the Bench that she had passed much of her time in Hedges's cabin during the voyage. She had also seen other women going down to the sailors' berths during the day. Although she couldn't be certain, she believed that they had also spent nights there. She agreed with Mary Long that the Surgeon Creagh knew what was happening but had not ordered her or the other women back to the prison room. He had simply urged them to be 'more circumspect' and to keep it from the priests because his living depended on his good character. In fact, she said, she and many other women had heard him say that he too would have a woman in his cabin if it were not for the priests. None of the women had complained about the way they were being treated by the sailors and she was sure that there had been no cause for complaint.

A few days later, the Bench reported to Macquarie that they were of the opinion that Prostitution did prevail on board the Ship throughout the Voyage from England. That due exertions were not made on the part of the Captain and officers to prevent the same; and that the matter of Charge, as against the Captain and Officers of the said Ship individually in that respect, is true and well founded in fact. Despite this finding, Mowat and Hedges as well as the other officers and crew of Janus all appear to have escaped penalty. With Mowat as master, the ship left Sydney on 26 July 1820 and, after thirteen weeks at sea, arrived at the Bay of Islands, New Zealand. There is no record of Mowat ever returning to Sydney.

I've read many similar stories about female convicts, with some reports totally denying that anything untoward happened onboard transportation ships. Others

Female Convicts being Transported

claim that prisoner prostitution was an everyday occurrence, pursued by the female prisoners themselves as a way to get money for their unknown futures. Some reports state that most female convicts transported were nothing but "whores, damned whores".

Yet, prostitution itself was not a transportable offence. Undoubtedly, some prostitutes *were* transported, but this was for other offences such as extortion or larceny. However, there is no reason or evidence to suggest that many of the women were prostitutes.

Whatever the truth is, having Isabella actually named in the enquiry makes it a much more meaningful report, to me. I can imagine the long journey. I can imagine the terrible, cramped and unhealthy conditions. I can imagine the uncertainty and the insecurity. Then, add to this a bunch of dirty, smelly, lecherous sailors, It doesn't bear thinking about.

So, the facts I knew were that Isabella was transported on the *Janus* and the date she arrived in New South Wales. I also knew when she left England – but that was all. Would it be enough? I had already found the ship's arrivals manifest that listed Isabella, but it gave no details of her offence or her place of conviction. I had nothing more to go on, and I still hadn't managed to link her to Ann Irvin.

Going over all the documents again, I noticed an entry for Mary, the wife of William Orr. Next to her name, it read: "Cumberland gaol delivery". And below this, Isabella was listed, but with no details – just a space. Could that be because her details were exactly the same as the line above, and it should really say "ditto"?

At least I had a clue. I eventually found the ship's indent, which should list every convict's first name, surname, age, offence and where sentenced. Once again, there was Mary, wife of William Orr (why didn't they just call her Mary Orr?) "Cumberland Gaol delivery" then the date she was sentences, 1st April 1819 as well as her sentence term - 7 years".

Again, Isabella was listed underneath, so maybe if I used 1st April 1819 as a clue, it would lead somewhere.

Searching Carlisle newspapers dated 1st April, 1819, I found a list of prisoners to be tried at the general gaol that day. The list included Elizabeth Irving, aged 23, for burglary, and Isabella Irving for "like offences."

10th April 1819 Carlisle Patriot

BURGLARY

ELIZABETH IRVING, aged 23, and ISABELLA IRVING, aged 29, charged upon the oath of George Tordiff, with having feloniously and burglariously broken open his dwelling house at Abbey Holm, and having stolen and taken away divers goods and chattels of the said Geo. Tordiff, &c.

Mr. LOSH opened the case, and stated that the property had been stolen from a kind of out house, attached to Mr. Tordiff's residence, which was only fastened by a latch.

Geo. Tordiff, the prosecutor, stated that he lived at Woolsty Hall, in Abbey Holm. On the night of the 21st December, a quantity of shirts, shifts, sheets &c. were stolen. On Tuesday he and Beck the constable procured a search warrant at Unerigg, and proceeded to Seaton, on approaching which, he saw Isabella Irving behind Hutchinson's house taking clothes from a hedge, and when she observed him she pulled them off much quicker. She gathered them up and went into a corner of a field and stuffed them into a conduit, from whence witness afterwards saw Messenger pull them. Witness is sure that these

153

clothes were his property. They went to the house of a person named Little where Elizabeth Irving lived, and found some more of the stolen clothes in a milk house. Elizabeth Irving was not there.

The prisoners were taken before a Magistrate. When Elizabeth was taken she said she cared nought for them "and could make a living if her hands were tied behind her back." On his cross examination, witness said the prisoners lived 15 or 16 miles from Woolsty Hall: Elizabeth Irving once lived near that place: he suspected Hutchinson and Little (two men) who have since absconded.

John Messenger went with Tordiff, Beck, and others to Seaton, on approaching which he saw some clothes hanging upon a hedge and people running about as if they (witness and party) had been noticed. Saw the clothes taken off the hedge by a woman who came out of Hutchinson's; she went to the corner of the house and looked as if watching their motions; she then went along a hedge, about 150 yards, and put the clothes into a conduit. Witness walked up to her, and she asked what was the matter; witness went and took out the clothes, and charged her with stealing them, but she denied it; she had put some grass and mould over them. They then went to John Little's, neither of the prisoners were there; Isabella was not in custody then. They found a checked shirt in a room that was locked. Mrs. Little at first said she had not the key, but afterwards produced it. Beck took all the articles in charge.

Geo. Robinson knows the prisoners. On the evening of 21st of December, he saw them going over Seaton Common leading a black mare belonging to John Little. Elizabeth got upon the pillion and went towards Dearham. The next morning between eight and nine he saw them again coming down to Seaton. Elizabeth was on the black mare, and Isabella was upon a grey pony belonging to William Hutchinson; the latter's horse was very dirty, and she had a bag under her; did not observe that Elizabeth had anything.

David Beck is a constable in Maryport. He went to Seaton and found the clothes as above stated. He saw Elizabeth apprehended behind Hutchinson's house. Witness said it would be better for her to tell if there were any more concerned. Her examination was taken down before the Magistrate.

Mary Tordiff, daughter of the prosecutor, identified the property. The clothes when stolen were wet; the house from which they were taken is in the yard, and under the same roof as the dwelling; the door was not locked, but was fastened with a latch.

His Lordship was of opinion that there was not sufficient evidence against Elizabeth to go to the Jury.

The Jury found Isabella guilty of stealing, but not in a dwelling house - and she was sentenced to seven years transportation.

I think the evidence from the newspaper report is sufficient to come to the conclusion that the Isabella Irving who was transported on the *Janus* was from Seaton, Cumberland. The fact that she was at the home of William Hutchinson is another important piece of evidence. This all suggests that Isabella Irving could be Ann Irving's daughter. However, it isn't 100% proof.

Modern genealogy relies more and more on DNA to generate clues, or to prove relationships. That's exactly what happened here. I had obtained DNA records from people who were descended from Isabella, as well as from descendants of William Hutchinson and Ann Irvin. Using group comparisons proved the relationship beyond doubt: the descendants of Isabella carried chromosomes which matched the descendants of Ann's son, George. They were definitely related. This proved that Isabella was Ann Irving's daughter. And if Isabella was Ann's daughter, then the Elizabeth Irving who was mentioned in the court case must be another of Ann's daughters, too. There was now clear proof that Ann Irving had had more children before George, Jane and Mary Ann – and perhaps there were more to discover, yet.

Some time after her transportation, Isabella married James Evans (another convict) on 28th February, 1823, at Castlereagh, New South Wales. The following year, she earned her Freedom Certificate. James and Isabella had two children, William and Hannah, in 1827 and 1829 respectively.

Isabella died on 17th October, 1835, sixteen years after arriving in Australia, at the age of 45.

Chapter 22

1838 - John Berry

Looking for John Berry had not been easy. I had completely lost track of him and his family after the baptism of his second son, Thomas, in 1836. Conventional searches of parish records, GRO records and census had thrown up nothing. I had managed to follow his two sons Hugh and Thomas, but John and his wife Ann had simply disappeared under the radar. I was beginning to presume that they had either died, or emigrated. Then, I tried something new. I'd subscribed to the British Newspaper Archive website, which had made copies of thousands of British Newspaper available, from 1710-1953. I hadn't had the subscription very long and I'd found it quite difficult to search. It was also very tedious, reading all the small print. Another problem was that the newspapers were so interesting that I got side-tracked too easily, enjoying myself, but wasting endless time reading about all kinds of social history that wasn't altogether relevant to my search.

Eventually, however, through sheer perseverance, I found something quite amazing! And something that – to be quite honest – changed me forever. I learned something of my own family history that was completely unexpected. (John Berry was the first criminal I found when researching my families history)

Westmorland Gazette 23rd June 1838

Appleby New Fair — Appleby new fair was held on Wednesday and Thursday, the 13th and 14th inst. The call for sheep was unusually brisk. Cattle in general sold well. Horses of a superior description sold very well and fetched good prices, while those of an inferior sort were hardly saleable; but taking the average, this fair was considered to be a very good one. There was as usual a large number of light fingered gentry in attendance. One person had his pocket eased of £9, another of his watch, and several other depredations were committed by that tribe. The gamblers were generally prohibited from acting in their capacity, having in the first instance been deprived of their materials by the judicious arrangement of Mr. Thomas Harrison, the high constable for the East Ward. In the course of Wednesday evening a general row took place with a gang of potters, tinkers, &c., which was attended by a serious disaster.

A person of the name John Berry came in contact with a person of the name Winter, when the former, finding himself inadequate to combat with the antagonist upon fair scientific principles, actually stabbed the unfortunate victim of his malice in the abdomen, with a knife. The villain was apprehended, and on Thursday examined and committed to the county gaol for further examination at a future period. Winter now lies in a dangerous state at the house of Mr James Richardson, the Cross Keys, in Battlebarrow, where every attention is paid by the medical gentlemen who were called upon to inspect the unfortunate individual. Hopes are entertained that he will recover.

I had found my 4-times great grandfather, John Berry.

John was held in prison at Appleby. The gaol had been built in 1771 to accommodate twenty inmates, both men and women, all in one communal cell. Prisoners were kept there awaiting judgement on their crimes. This might mean them being sentenced to flogging, deportation or hanging. The gaol had a formal full-time police force established there in 1820.

John remained in gaol until he appeared at the Westmorland Summer Assizes in Appleby Court House on Thursday August 2nd, 1838.

Westmorland Gazette 11th August 1838

The commission for holding the Summer Assizes for the County of Westmorland was opened with the usual forms, on Thursday in last week, at Appleby, by Mr. Baron Anderson, who afterwards, according to custom, took up his lodgings in Appleby Castle. Mr. Baron Anderson was next morning joined by Mr. Justice Williams, who had been detained at Carlisle, and half-past ten o'clock they both proceeded under the escort of the Magistrates of the town, and gentlemen of the county, to the Church of St. Lawrence, where an appropriate sermon was delivered on the occasion by the Rev. Mr Threlkeld, from the 14th verse of the 34th Psalm, "Depart from evil and do good." Divine service having been concluded, the Judges at twelve o'clock proceeded to the Court House, where Mr. Justice Williams presided in the Crown Court and Mr. Baron Anderson in the Nisi Prius Court.

John Berry was now in court, facing an indictment for Unlawful and Malicious Stabbing. Before the session commenced, the judge addressed the jurors:

Gentlemen, there is another case, I am sorry to say, marked apparently with a degree of savageness and malignity that rarely occurs in this quarter; it is the case of one man stabbing and cutting another. You are aware of the alteration in the law with respect to this species of crime, Formerly. before the act commonly known as Lord Ellenborough's Act was passed, in such cases as it was ascertained that stabbing or injuring another took place after a quarrel ensued and the blood was heated, whatever the extent of malignity attending it, the circumstances of the blood being heated formed a reason for acquittal: but now the state of the law is altered and if from the depositions you discover evidence to show that there has been malignity, whether the result of temporary excitement or not, I recommend you to find for a trial, and under the highest designation of the crime which the act of parliament prescribes. If it appears to you that one of the two men who were fighting, drew a knife and inflicted wounds on the body of his antagonist, I have no difficulty in saying that, according to the present act, the crime will come under it.

The Judge had issued a clear warning that if John was found guilty, he would face a very serious penalty. The case took most of the afternoon, with several witnesses being called.

Perhaps the best way to give a clear picture of the proceedings is to transcribe, verbatim, from the Westmorland Gazette. There is clearly an error in the report, but I put that down to the court secretary's error, and it would not have affected the outcome.

Unlawful and Malicious Stabbing

John Bery[sic], aged 31, was indicted on the charge of unlawfully and maliciously, stabbing, cutting and wounding Robert Winter, at New Fair Hill, in the Parish of Bondgate, on the 13th day of June last.

Mr. Ramshay appeared for the prosecution, and Mr. Rawlinson for the prisoner.

Having briefly stated the case, Mr. Rawlinson called the following witnesses:-

Robert Winter, sworn. — This was the part wounded; he came into court, supporting himself on a staff, and appeared to be in a very weakly state. — I was at New Fair Hill on the 13th day of June last; I was drinking in a tent; the prisoner came in after it was dark; I don't recollect that he said anything when he came in; but he called us, my fore-elders, "a hanged and gibbetted crewe." I then went out on the road, and we got to bats, and then he stabbed me.

By the Court — We went out on the road to fight, and he stabbed me.

By Mr. Rawlinson — He stabbed me in the bottom of the belly.

Cross examined by Mr. Ramshay, — The witness leant with his head on his hand, and upon Mr. Ramshay's desiring him to turn and hold himself up, he said he was unable, and called for water to wet his mouth.

Mr. Ramshay. — Turn your head this way and answer me.

Mr. Rawlinson and others. — The witness cannot hold up his head, he is in a weak state.

Mr. Ramshay, — It may be for what I know be a sham.

Mr Ramshay to the witness, — What are you?

Witness. — I make tins — I am a Tinker; I travel about the country and have no settled home; I sleep at a hedge-back; I had never a quarrel with Bery; I was not in his company before, except on that day; I had seen the prisoner that day before he came to the tent in the evening, but had not been in his company; I did not charge the prisoner with cheating about swapping a horse with my father; I never called him a cheat; I don't recollect hearing my father speak of it. The prisoner was first in the tent on the day in question, about darkening; I went into the tent and found him; some people were with me — my father, my brother Collin and Jamie Lowther (a laugh); I can't say about Bob Miller. The prisoner was with Allan and Hutchinson his brother-in-law; I don't know whom the quarrel began with; I was drunkish — I was not sober, I could walk on my feet at the time; I don't remember what was said; I didn't hear anything said at the time. Prisoner called us "a hanged and gibbetted crewe;" these were the first words; I can't tell if anything was said to him; I can't say whether our party abused the prisoner's party; I did not see Collin strike the prisoner; I went out of the tent quietly; we were not turned out of the tent for quarrelling; I don't recollect being turned out.

By the Court — There was a quarrel when we got out of the tent.

Cross-examination continued. — Prisoner's wife did not take him away; I was on the road when I was stabbed; the distance from the place where I was stabbed to the tent was one hundred yards; I can't say whether the distance is ten or one hundred yards; I was stabbed immediately upon going out of the tent; when he said we were "a hanged and gibbetted crewe," I followed him and his wife; I never had a knife that day; I didn't cut the prisoner's wife's arm; I had no knife carrying about with me; I don't recollect calling names — can't swear I didn't call names: I can't swear I didn't strike her with my hand; I might have struck her with my hand; I don't recollect that; I and Collin punched the prisoner when he was down; I don't recollect who struck the first blow; I can't talk to you (querulously).

By Mr. Rawlinson. — I and my brother Collin left the tent when the quarrel took place.

By the Court. — I saw the prisoner in two tents that day.

By Mr. Rawlinson. — His wife and somebody else took the prisoner away from the tent where the quarrel began, and I and my brother Collin went to another tent; the next time we saw the prisoner was in the second tent; he came to me and used the words "a hanged and gibbetted crewe."

Robert Gordon was called, but not appearing, the Judge ordered his recognisances to be estreated.

Robert Miller sworn and examined. — I recollect the fair day, and I was in the tent with Winter on the night; I recollect the prisoner coming into the tent; I was not at the beginning of the consarn[sic], I was in at the last; the prisoner had some mischief with Robert Winter; the prisoner said, when coming down into the tent, he would be revenged of Winter; when he came in he called Winter's family an awkward name, and they (the prisoner and Winter) went out and fell together; they wrestled together and fell, and when Winter got up he put his hand to his side and said, "Bery has stabbed me." I saw something fall from Bery's hand, but I don't know what it was; I saw a knife found in the water.

Cross-examined, — This happened when it was not very dark, but dusky; I and the prosecutor had been in the tent, and I heard the prisoner come down the road; he might be as far distant from the tent when I heard him as between this (the witness box) and that wall (pointing to the court room front wall); the tent was a long one; there was not many in the tent; about half-a-dozen — a man here, a man there. I did not see twenty persons on the fair hill; the words the prisoner said were "I'll be revenged on the Winters;" I was not surprised at the words when I heard them, as I knew it was not my fate; I and Bob Miller were going about at the fair in the course of the day; I was sitting in the tent in the evening — had some ale, but I was quite sober; Winter was toxicated[sic] in liquor (a laugh). There were three or four of us in the tent — old Robert Winter, the father, and myself, and young Jamie Lowther. The prisoner came alone by himself, and soon after, another man came. The prisoner first began; I can't say the words he spoke, but they were not friendly; he was in a threatening situation (position); I don't know what he began about; the prisoner said he would be revenged; I did not hear further; our party were not turned out of the tent; I saw no fighting between Winter and the prisoner but their wrestling one another down; I know nothing about a former quarrel, or about a horse; I never heard about the horse; I did not hear Robert Winter speak of a bargain. The fight took place about nine to ten yards from the tent; I was close by and saw the prisoner's wife, but I did not see him and his wife go together; I saw the prisoner go up the fair hill as soon as he got shot of the mischief ; I did not see his wife at the fight; I did not see Winter knock the prisoner down, both went down together; when Winter said he was stabbed both were down; I did not hear of any quarrel, nor do I know what they quarrelled about; I can't say if there was a crowd about when they fought; there were some people about — perhaps nine or ten; I never saw the prosecutor strike the prisoners wife; I'm a little if anything a friend of the prosecutor's.

William Strickland, sworn — I was on the ground and saw the prisoner at the fair and Winter also; I saw them quarrelling outside of a tent; and I saw them when the man was stabbed. The prisoner when going away from the tent looked over his shoulder and said something, then they got to close quarters, and both fell, and Winter cried out he was stabbed; Robert Gordon was present at the time. I found a knife in some water close to the spot; the knife was open, the blade was stuck in the ground and the haft was above the water; I gave the knife to the constable.

Cross-examined — I heard words spoken by the prisoner when he went away; there were two tents and a road in the middle between them; the water was close to the road side. The first thing I saw was the prisoner going away from Winter, before he (the prisoner) spoke the words; when he spoke, he turned round; I saw his wife who tried to make peace, but I did not see Winter strike her. I saw the wife next day, her arm was tied up. Bob Miller was about three or four yards from the prisoner and Winter when they fought; I was near them when they got together, but Miller was nearer than me; I saw the knife; Winter shouted out, went up and down crying, "I am stabbed." I did not see Winter with a clasp knife; it might be between ten and eleven o'clock when they fought. I gave the knife to Thomas Dover the constable.

Thomas Dover, sworn — I am a constable; I got the knife which I now produce, from the witness.

William Winter, brother of the prosecutor being called and not answering to his name, his recognisances were ordered to be estreated.

F.M. Dinwoodie, sworn — I am a surgeon; I was called to attend Winter when he was stabbed; I found a wound in the abdomen, and one in the haunch (both on the left side); a knife like the one now shown would produce the wounds. I considered Winter's life in danger.

By Mr. Ramshay — I was applied to attend the prisoner's wife, and found her wounded in the arm; it was by a stab; it might be by a clasp knife, it was a wound in the elbow; a man might have stabbed himself in a struggle, but considering that two wounds were inflicted I certainly don't think it too likely.

By Mr. Rawlinson — My reason for thinking it improbable is that both wounds were on the left side, which is not likely a knife in his own right hand would inflict. I dressed Winter's wife's arm.

By the Court — Winter's wife said she had received the wound in separating two people in a scuffle.

This concluded the evidence.

Mr. Ramshay then addressed the jury in behalf of the prisoner — The learned council adverted to the absence of the parties who had been bound over to appear as witnesses on the trial; he called particular attention to the circumstance of the prosecutor's brother not appearing, and expressed his impression that the witness, whose evidence might have borne strongly against the prosecutor, had been kept back by the prosecutor himself. It was singular, he observed, that the prosecutor's own brother should absent himself, and it looked extremely suspicious. The facts of the case, he conceived, had not been presented in their due light by the witness. There was a man (pointing to the prisoner) who had been represented as going singly into a tent to meet four others; it was seldom that one man would venture to meet four men in a hostile attitude, and the circumstance of Bery's facing four men was at least highly improbable.

Mr. Ramshay next animadverted strongly upon the manner in which the prosecutor had given his evidence; when cross-examined he turned his head aside as if labouring under great weakness; but it might probably arise from another motive. Winter could remember all that had a tendency to favour himself, but as to what might turn out as evidence against him, he could recollect nothing. On the one side he was sober, on the other he was not sober. He (Mr. Ramshay) could not believe that he had spoken the truth. The learned Council then made an allusion to Winter's mode of life; the class to which he belonged were not usually men of good repute, and he had no doubt that the whole gang of Tinkers would be ready to come forward to support him in whatever statement he might make.

Mr. Justice Williams then recalled Mr. Dinwoodie, surgeon, and put a few questions to him regarding Winter's state of health, to which the following are answers:-

Winter I should think is out of danger; I know he is extremely weak; I think the weakness he shows here is not altogether feigned; he was kept six weeks on a very low diet, and was in bed generally.

His Lordship now summed up, directing the attention of the jury not so much to the origin of the quarrel as to the act of stabbing. His Lordship requested them to consider whether there was in witness's manner any proof that his weakness was feigned to make a convenient escape from being too closely examined — whether it was the languor of disease or the languor of design. He next averted to Winter's denial of having carried a knife in his hand on the day the quarrel happened — to his acknowledgement "I was drunkish — I could walk on my legs;" and recommended the jury to take this into consideration as a point of considerable importance, as it referred to the infliction of the wound.

His Lordship then explained such of Miller's evidence as bore on the case, and concluded by laying some stress upon the unembarrassed manner in which Strickland stated the facts. The Jury having consulted for some time, returned a verdict finding the prisoner Guilty.

His Lordship then after a short, but able address, sentenced the prisoner to be transported beyond the seas for the term of his natural life.

The prisoner's appearance was callous during all the time of the trial; but his wife, mother, father, and other relatives had assembled at the door of the Court House, anxiously awaiting the result, and upon hearing his fate, his wife fainted, and his father gave vent to his feelings in loud agonised cries of grief. The scene altogether was of a most heart-rending description.

So, that was that. My 4-times great grandfather, John Berry, was found guilty, and was to be transported across the seas to the penal colonies in Australia.

Just over three weeks later, the following was reported:

Kendal Mercury 25th August 1838

On Sunday evening last, Mr. Thwaites, Governor of the County Gaol, left Appleby with five convicts. John Wharton, for sheep stealing. John Berry, for cutting and maiming, William Pearson, for burglary, William Hewitson for burglary, and John Bateman, for larceny (his third offence) for the Ganymede Hulk, lying off Woolwich. He proceeded forthwith to York, thence to Hull, and from thence to London.

The Prison Hulk Ganymede

164

The journey to Woolwich would have been taken by Black Mariah to York; then, on the following day, the same method of transport would have taken them to Hull. From there, they would have travelled on board a coaster to London. Transporting them by sea for the main distance was seen as the most secure way of moving prisoners. However, many convicts were transported from Carlisle to London by road at a cost of £15 4s 0d. per person. The gaoler would normally choose the cheapest method.

Searches of Criminal Registers show that John arrived on the prison hulk *Ganymede* on 23rd August, 1838. The hulk register shows:

Prisoner 5234, John Bery, Age 31

Crime-Cutting and Stabbing, Convicted Appleby 2nd August, Sentence Life, wife and two children [Hugh and Thomas].

I later found that his wife was pregnant at the time of John's conviction, giving birth to a daughter, Ann, the following March. The register goes on to show that John could neither read nor write, his occupation was given as "Farmer's Labourer" and he was to be disposed of onboard the *Parkfield* on 4th May, 1839, bound for New South Wales.

John appeared to have a little bit of luck on his side. John Wharton, who was convicted at Appleby for sheep stealing on the same day, and who had travelled with him to London, was given prisoner number 5233 and therefore would be chained up next to John in the *Ganymede* prison hulk on the Thames whilst awaiting transportation. Later research shows the Wharton and Berry families intermarrying, so there is a fair chance that they already knew each other. They would both wear their prison uniform with their number clearly showing, since that would be how they were referred to from then, on. They would then travel together on the *Parkfield* to Australia. John Wharton left behind a wife and seven children.

Ganymede was just one of around sixty ships used for this purpose. The *Ganymede* had started life as the French naval frigate, *Hebe*, captured by the British fleet in 1809, and converted to a prison hulk in 1819, when she joined the Thames prison fleet as just one of many prison hulks on the river. Convicts who had been sentenced to be transported were incarcerated in these hulks until space on a transport ship could be found.

Ganymede was moored off the south shore of the Thames at Woolwich. The area known as the "Woolwich Warren" was a maze of workshops, warehouses, wood-yards, barracks, foundries and firing ranges.

165

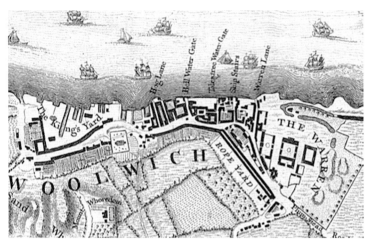

Woolwich Warren

Despite the low-cost food, clothing and accommodation provided, it was considered expensive to keep a prisoner onboard a hulk, so prisoners were put to work, effectively to earn their keep. Their main work was dredging the river and maintaining its banks by driving posts into them to prevent erosion. As Woolwich arsenal was being developed, prisoners also dug canals and built walls around the arsenal. Convicts were worked hard for ten hours each day in summer and seven in winter, when the daylight was limited.

James Hardy Vaux was a prisoner on the hulk *Retribution* around the same time as John Berry, whilst waiting for transportation to New South Wales. He recorded that:

> *Every morning at seven o'clock, all the convicts capable of work, or, in fact, all who are capable of getting into the boats, are taken ashore to the Warren, in which the Royal Arsenal and other public buildings are situated, and there employed at various kinds of labour; some of them very fatiguing and while so employed, each gang of sixteen or twenty men is watched and directed by a fellow called a guard. These guards are commonly of the lowest class of human beings, wretched devoid of feeling; ignorant in the extreme, brutal by nature, and rendered tyrannical and cruel by the consciousness of the power they possess. They invariably carry a large and ponderous stick, with which, without the smallest provocation, they fell an unfortunate convict to the ground, and frequently repeat their blows long after the poor fellow is insensible.*

Many prisoners spent months, if not years, onboard the hulks, waiting for transportation. Sickness and disease were rife, and mortality rates were around 30%. Prisoners who died were buried in mass unmarked graves in the arsenal's grounds – and burials were not recorded.

It must have been a relief to John, when on 12th May, 1839, he was finally put onboard the *Parkfield* at Sheerness for the first part of the voyage to Deptford to pick up passengers; then to sail across the seas to Australia. The *Parkfield*'s captain was J.T. Whiteside and the ship's surgeon was Alexander Neill.

Whilst John was imprisoned onboard the *Ganymede*, several letters had been sent to the Secretary of State for the Colonies, pleading for clemency for John. One letter, dated September 6th, 1838, written by Father Aglionby of the Nunnery, Penrith acted as a cover letter to introduce further pleas for leniency:

> *My Lord*
>
> *I have been requested to lay before your lordship the accompanying papers, respecting John Berry, a convict sentenced to transportation for life at the last Assizes for the County of Westmorland.*
>
> *I have the honour to be, My Lord, your Lordship's most Dedicated Servant,*
>
> *Fr Aglionby*

Enclosed with this, there were two more letters. The first, read:

> *The undersigned beg to state that they have for many years known John Berry who was in Appleby prison under sentence of transportation for life, for cutting Robert Winter with a knife, and that they believe him to have ever been a man of placeable and quiet character, and were surprised to hear of the present charge against him, and that they would gladly have of the sentence against him being reduced as low as possible, particularly as he has a wife and two children in great distress, and his father a blind man depending on him for his support, they therefore kindly beg that the sentence may be commuted to one of imprisonment.*
>
> *Edward Bell, for the number of 26 years upwards; for a well disposed person to my belief.*
>
> *John Mullender, has known the above named John Bery for sixteen years*
>
> *Thomas Snowden, Black Smith*
>
> *John Donely, I have known him 18 yrs*

John Burgess, I have known him 10

Andrew Smith, Shoemaker. Known John Berry for 10 years

Robinson Utner, horse keeper. Known John Berry for 3 years

James Smith, Chair Maker. I never knew him to be anything but a peaceful and industrious man

I never knew any thing of him these thirteen years but industrious and quiet. Henry Carlisle

Colin Bateman, Chair Maker, knew him 10 years.

I was very surprised to read the second accompanying letter – which had been sent by Robert Winter, the man John had fought with and stabbed – and the reason he was convicted.

I Robert Winter do solemnly declare that I really believe that John Berry who was in the prison at Appleby under sentence of transportation for life for stabbing me, I really believe he had neither spite nor malice against me for we were always particular friend with each other and was drinking together good friends the morning that the misfortune happened and that the quarrel arose out of our being fighting and intoxication in the cause of the day. Therefore I most humbly implore that the sentence against John Berry may be mitigated to a term of imprisonment as I am recovered from the wounds and is as well as ever I was in my life for which I most humbly and sincerely pray.

John Cass witness to the above

His mark - X - Robert Winter.

That's quite a turnaround. It's so hard to believe that the man who wrote this was the same man challenging John Berry in court, barely a month earlier. This letter, compared with his statements and conduct during the court case is so contradictory. Here he is, saying they were great friends, and that alcohol was to blame for his bad luck – and that he's now completely recovered and never felt better in his life.

But – it was all too late to claim it had been a flash in the pan, now. John had been convicted. He was locked up in shackles on the prison hulk. The letters made no difference, and on September 21st, 1838, the pleas for clemency were turned down. John Berry was on his way to the colonies.

The *Parkfield*, which had been built in the Isle of Man in 1833 weighed in at 496

I Robert Winter do Solemnly declare that I really believe that John Berry who was in the prison at Appleby under Sentence of Transportation for life for Stabbing me I really believe he had neither Spite or malice against me for we were always particular friends with each other and was drinking together good friends the morning that the misfortune happened and that the quarrel arose out of our being fighting and intoxication in the Course of the day therefore I most humbly implore that the Sentence against John Berry may be mitigated to a term of imprisonment as I am recovered from the wounds and is as well as ever I was in my life for which I most Humbly and Sincerely pray

John Carr Witness to the above

his mark + Robert Winter

Plea for Clemency by Robert Winter

tons. She left Sheerness on 15th May, 1839, with 240 convicts on board; 51 of whom had been given life sentences. Others aboard included Captain Rice, Ensign Kelly and 29 rank and file of the 31st Regiment; as well as six women passengers and nine children, who embarked at Deptford. The journey took 109 days, and the ship arrived in Port Jackson on 1st September, 1839.

Ship's surgeon, Alexander Neill, kept a medical journal from 1st May until 7th September. The first entry read:

On Saturday 4th May, 1839, the ship dropped down to Woolwich and fifty prisoners were embarked from the Justitia and fifty from the Ganymede hulk, apparently in very good health. One of the men had been subject to epilepsy from childhood and has had several very severe attacks since embarkation, from his being a great nuisance to the other prisoners I did apply to have him removed but we sailed before an answer arrived. After the embarkation of the Woolwich prisoners we proceeded the same evening to Sheerness by steam and when we arrived on Sunday morning the 5th I reported the ship's arrival to Sir J. Hill. On Monday I went to Chatham and examined the prisoners, rejecting several who were labouring under diseases and I was rather astonished to find symptoms of scurvy in one case as bad as I have seen at sea, purple spongy gums, contraction of the muscle of the legs and macula on the chest and arms; this case only shows the great necessity for a surgeon commencing a four month voyage to be accordingly particular in his examination of prisoners. One hundred and fifty prisoners were embarked at Sheerness from the Fortitude at Chatham, making in all 240.

The journey had been relatively uneventful and left most of those aboard reasonably healthy. The ship did not encounter a single gale on the voyage and there were no prisoners on the sick list; nor had any died on the voyage. Further, in his summary of the voyage, Alexander Neill made the following observation:

I beg further to state that in two voyages in convict ships, I have found dogs a very great nuisance, not only making dirt about the decks but in one case tearing down the ventilation near the beds; and another great objection to their being on board a ship crowded with people is that they are liable to be trampled on accidentally by the prisoners, which in the part of the owner of the dog, nine times out of ten be called wilful; and greatly likely to lean to discussion amongst those whose duties should go hand in hand.

The Sydney Herald reported that:

The convicts were inspected on Monday, 2nd September, by the Board of Health Officers, who were highly gratified at the cleanliness of the vessel and good order of everyone on board. Mr. Neill, the surgeon, was congratulated on his return to the colony by his many respectable friends, all of whom were happy to hear of his arrival without the death of a single individual. This is the gentleman who so politely volunteered his services on the occasion of the "John Barry" being placed in quarantine some years back, and was very near to losing his own life.

On Saturday, 7th September, the convicts of the Parkfield were inspected by the Governor, Sir George Gipps, in Hyde Park Barracks. His Excellency told the second-class men that it was impossible that he could do anything for them for two years after their arrival, but after that period, all who behaved themselves well would receive the indulgence of being assigned to private service. The first-class men, he said, must remain in government employment for six months, after which they would be assigned out, if they deserved it. At their work, they would be divided into gangs of ten or twelve men, who would be made responsible for each other's conduct, so that if they have a bad man amongst them it would be in their interest to inform their superintendent of it, and the man would be removed.

Willingness at their work, he particularly impressed upon them, as being necessary if they wished to obtain any indulgence. Three men who attempted to escape from the ship after arrival in harbour were placed in the second class. Among the prisoners were sixteen soldiers, for different offences, among whom were four soldiers of the 67th regiment, who were transported for manslaughter in killing a marine in a drunken fray at Chatham.

In an advertisement soon after arrival, the Parkfield was said to be well known as one of the fastest sailing vessels carrying British Colours and could also stow a fair cargo. She could be chartered by contacting Captain Whiteside on board or agents Dunlop & Co. in Queen Street.

All had gone well, the surgeon was praised for maintaining health; as was the ship commended for its cleanliness (in spite of the presence of dogs soiling the deck...), and the usual briefings were given. The ship was now ready for offers to take cargo back to England on the return voyage.

Reading the indent of prisoners who arrived on the *Parkfield* gave me much more of an insight into John. His indent number was 217 (out of 240 prisoners). Again, it is confirmed that he was neither able to read nor write, and his religion was Protestant.

Interestingly, the indent states that he had 3 children. I already knew that John's wife was pregnant when he was convicted and sent to the hulks in August 1838. His daughter, Ann, was baptised at Torpenhow on 10th March, 1839, so somehow the authorities in Australia knew of the birth, I wondered if John knew.

John's "native place" is shown as Annandale, a region of what is now Dumfries and Galloway, running north-south from the English border, following the river Annan. This was the first indication that John could have been Scottish. His occupation is shown as "Labourer". The indent confirms that his offence was "Cutting and Maiming" and that he was tried at Westmorland Assizes, sentenced on 2nd August, 1838 to transportation for life, and it shows that John had no previous convictions.

The indent goes on to give a physical description of John – which for the first time helps me to visualise how he might have looked. He was 5' 5 and 3/4" tall, with a brown complexion, dark brown hair and chestnut eyes. His distinguishing features are listed as: "Diagonal scar under outer corner of right eye, another outside left eye, indented scar on left jaw, lost part of left ear, small mole on lower left arm, two scars on ball of left thumb, another on back of same, scar on left knee." And most surprisingly: "Legs Hairy".

Going over these details listed in his arrival indent and writing them down here has been extremely poignant for me. I suppose that, for the first time, John Berry, my 4x great grandfather had just become a real person. His story was about to get even more emotionally touching.

Searching convict records available online produced two or three relevant records, but they revealed nothing new to me. Nor did they give any insight into

John's early years in Australia.

I searched Australian newspapers for any mention of John Berry/Bery, and again, I came across nothing.

Finally, I checked convict death records and, sadly, I read of John's death.

Berry John, no age shown, arrived on Parkfield, date of burial 4th August 1842 at Haywood district. Remarks, Hanged Himself.

I was saddened and sickened by this remark. What had led John to take his own life? Looking for more information led me to search for a coroner's inquest report – which I found. It simply stated that an inquest for John Berry at Parramatta on 10th August 1842 found that the cause of death was "Falo-de-se", which is Latin for "Felon of himself" – suicide.

Why John chose this route, we'll never know. I'd like to think that he was not a hardened criminal. He had suffered the worst possible outcome from a drunken day out at Appleby Fair, probably one of the few social days out in what was generally a hard and miserable life. He had sustained imprisonment and hard labour on the hulks, a long voyage and three years in a strange land, committed to a hard life of more labour. I believe he probably missed his wife and family and realised that transportation for life meant exactly that. There was no way he would ever see his family again, and he could take no more, so he chose to beat the system by ending his life.

Unfortunately, since John had killed himself, he could not be buried in consecrated ground. Therefore, there is no marker or record of where John finally came to rest.

That should have been the end of my research into my 4-times great grandparents, but there were still a couple of loose ends to be tied up.

What happened to his wife, Ann? And what happened to the daughter he never knew?

Chapter 23
1847 - Thomas Berry

Researching John Berry's story had been so fascinating that the whole Berry family now had my full attention. I'd never anticipated finding a story like John's in my family's history. I have to admit that, at first, it was a bit of a shock, but now, I was absolutely hooked. Criminals and convicts sounded much more exciting, to me, than a family full of vicars, teachers or bank managers (not that there's anything wrong with those). They also provided a richer range and source of detailed historical information and records than other families' ancestors: there was much more written about scallywags in the newspapers, since they tended to make more news.

Now that I was committed to this family line, I had to do more research. My main objective was to find John Berry's children and wife, to see how their lives fared; but I must confess that I also hoped to uncover more colourful stories, in the process.

It didn't take long to go through parish registers, and find that John and his wife, Ann, had five children: Jane, Mary, Hugh, Thomas and Ann.

I'd followed the life of my 3-times great grandfather, Thomas Berry, and I thought I knew his story; but just in case he turned out to be a rogue, too, I thought he should be investigated again. As far as the other children went, I knew very little, or even nothing at all.

The first place I looked was the England and Wales Criminal Register. This was available online through my subscription to a genealogical website. I simply typed in "Thomas Berry" and "Cumberland" and – hey, presto! There was an entry.

On August 2nd, 1847, Thomas Berry was indicted for assault on an individual – in fact, for malicious stabbing. Thomas was found guilty and sentenced to two months in gaol. Like father, like son! Was Thomas following in his father's footsteps? Using this basic information, I searched the British Newspaper Archive a fantastic online resource – until I found the following news report of the Summer Assizes:

THOMAS BERRY (17), charged with having stabbed Gerrard Steel, in the parish of Bridekirk, on 1st day of April last.

Mr James appeared for the prosecution, and after stating the case to the Jury called Gerrard Steel. - examined by Mr. Oliphant.

I was servant with Mr. Mossop of Woodside. I remember the 1st of April last. I got up at six o'clock. I slept that night with the prisoner. When I got up I went and fed the horses. I then went into the byre to fodder the cattle. Prisoner was then in the hay-loft. I was cleaning out the byre, and prisoner was standing looking at me. I told him to get the "muck" cleaned up. He said he would suit himself. I then took my hand and pushed him off. He then kicked me with his foot. I then shoved him back again and he fell. He then got up and took the coal-rake and said he would fell me. I took hold of the rake and took it from him, and gave him a kick back again. He then got up and took out his knife and said he would stick me. He stabbed me twice and I kept his hand back. I told him he was not worth bothering with when he would do something such as that. I then turned round and he struck at me in the side with the knife. I then shoved him behind the door. He was then shouting, and I put my thumb into his mouth and told him he might bite it off as he had stabbed me in the side.

I then turned from him and put some "muck" into the barrow. I then could not stand. I had to go and lay down between two beasts. The wound bled a good deal. It was on my left side. I was then taken into the house and put to bed. I remained there about a week. The doctor visited me three times.

Cross-examined by Mr. Ramshay [the same person who was prosecutor at his father's trial, nine years earlier!]

I do not know how old prisoner is. I am 21. I believe there are four or five stone between us in weight. The prisoner told me he would not do something that I told him, and I shoved him off. I shoved him down once and he fell in the dirt.

Mary Cuthbertson - I was servant with Mr. Mossop on 1st of April last. I went into the byre early that morning. Prisoner and last witness were there quarrelling. I heard the prosecutor say he would make the prisoner

175

work, and he replied he would not, he was not his master. The boy took the coal-rake to strike last witness with. The man then took hold of his hand and knocked him down. The prisoner got up and said that he would stab witness. I saw the knife in prisoner's hand. He stabbed three times at last witness and third time the knife went into him. The prosecutor put some "muck" into the barrow, and he then went and laid down between the cows. I went and woke my master and mistress. We then carried him into the house.

George Reay - I am a surgeon in Maryport. I was called to see the prosecutor on the 1st of April. He had a wound in his left side. It was about an inch in length. The wound did not appear dangerous, but the situation was so. It was about the seventh rib near the arm. The wound bled a little when I saw it. I considered it necessary for him to keep his bed. The wounds healed by the first intention. It healed very favourably. The wound only bled a little when I saw it, but it had previously bled a good deal.

Mr. Ramshay addressed the Jury at some length, contending that the prisoner had been influenced by passion, and that there had been great provocation on the part of prosecutor for the offence, and the question for them to consider was whether the lad had been guilty of the act with a felonious intention, or merely with the intention of violently assaulting him.

The learned Judge summed up the evidence with great care. The Jury immediately found the prisoner Guilty of assault only.

Sentence: Two calendar months with hard labour.

Considering his father's sentence, Thomas had got off extremely lightly, for stabbing someone!

Looking over all the information I had found on Thomas, this story threw up a big anomaly: how old was he, really? The newspaper report showed his age as seventeen – but this was impossible! I had already found his baptism record in October 1836, which – if he was born shortly before that, would make him eleven at the time of the trial. However, I'd learned never to presume that the year of baptism was the same as the year of birth. It's safe to say we could easily add one, two or, at a push, even three years. This means that he was probably between twelve and fourteen when he went to gaol. I think this assumption can be supported by other comments in the news report:

> *"I do not know how old prisoner is. I am 21. I believe there are four or five stone between us in weight".*

For this to be worthy of comment in the report, Thomas must have been significantly smaller than Gerrard Steel. Four or five stones' difference in weight is 25kg to 30kg – a huge difference!

Likewise, in Mary Cuthbertson's witness account, she made the following statement:

> *"The boy took the coal-rake to strike last witness with. The man then took hold of his hand and knocked him down".*

Here, she was referring to Thomas as a boy, while she saw Gerrard Steel as a man. I think, again, this clearly shows that Thomas was significantly younger than Gerrard.

Combining all the facts, I think my assumption of him being twelve to fourteen years old at the time is probably fair. Perhaps this physical difference between his slight, boyish figure as the attacker and his much heavier victim had some influence over his sentencing. In addition to the fact that this was apparently his first offence.

Still, Thomas gets 2 months' hard labour – at such a young age. Putting it into context, his father was transported for life for the same offence, nine years earlier. Maybe Thomas thought himself very lucky.

Searching through parish registers by using the International Genealogical Index, I'd come across several children who had been born to a Thomas Berry and his wife, Martha; the first being Ann, who was registered in 1855. This looked to be a likely candidate for Thomas's first child. Civil registration of births, marriages and deaths in England and Wales had begun on 1 July 1837, which made it a lot easier for my research of this generation – so I ordered a copy of her birth certificate, to find out more details.

When it arrived, it read:

> *6th September 1855. Born Townhead, Penrith. Ann, Girl. Father - Thomas Berry, Mother - Martha Berry formerly Hutchinson, Occupation of father - Basket Maker.*

What a lot of great information from a single birth, now that they were certified!

Since Martha was "Berry formerly Hutchinson" I decided to track down details of their marriage. Except I couldn't find any General Register Office reference to Thomas and Martha's marriage using normal methods or parish church records. The Berry's and Hutchinson's lived close to the border with Scotland and Scottish law didn't require marriage banns to be read for three weeks prior to the marriage, making the ceremony almost instant. Most people are aware that weddings took place at the Blacksmith's Shop, Gretna Green; but they may not be aware that there were several other places people could get married quickly and easily.

So, I decided to look through the marriage records from Allison's Bank Toll House at Gretna Green, copies of these records are held by Carlisle archives, but they are not indexed. which meant a slow search, page by page. Allison's Bank Toll House was the first house across the border into Scotland, and enterprising tollhouse keeper, John Murray, offered the lowest price weddings and registration in the area. I knew from previous viewings of the records that Travelling families liked to use this establishment.

Using daughter Ann's birth as a reference point, I went back in time by nine months and started searching from the end of 1854. It didn't take much time before I found the marriage record for Thomas and Martha, dated 14th November, 1854.

My overall picture of Thomas was building, and I went back to the newspapers hoping for more.

It didn't take long until I found a report of Thomas being convicted again, along with his brother, Hugh. This was published in the Kendal Mercury, dated 13th October 1855, just over a month after Thomas and Martha's marriage.

Kendal Mercury 13th October 1855

Magistrates office, Penrith, Oct 13. - (Before Thomas Scott, Esq.) - Thomas Berry, Hugh Berry and M Davidson, were brought up in custody of P.C. Coulthard and charged with forming an encampment at Wickerfield, in the township of Kings Meaburn, and thereby threatening to invade the hedges and hen roosts of the neighbouring farmers.

Two months each as rogues and vagabonds.

Reading this didn't just mildly interest me, in the way other similar articles had done. For the first time, I felt emotionally involved. In fact, I felt downright angry. Two months in prison, probably involving hard labour, just for living outdoors?

As I mentioned earlier, gypsy caravans or "vardos" didn't exist until the mid-1850s and even then, only the wealthiest could afford them. Thomas and Hugh

Allison's Bank Toll House,
Parish of Gretna, Scotland,
14 th November 1854

We _Thomas Berry_

Residing in the Parish of _Plumpth_ _in the County_

of _Cumberland_ and _Martha Hutchinson_

Residing in the Parish of _Seaton_ _in the County of_

Cumberland _do hereby acknowledge_

ourselves to be Married Persons, in testimony whereof we have requested

Janet Murray Gretna _and_

John Murray Gretna _to Sign this,_

as to the genuineness of our Signatures. _and. Marriage._

Thomas + Berry
Martha + Hutchinson
Before John Murray
Janet Murray Gretna } _Witnesses._
John Murray Gretna

Thomas Berry's marriage to Martha Hutchinson

would have made an "encampment" by building a bender tent from long lengths of flexible branches pushed into the ground and bent over to form a frame they could drape with some kind of covering to keep out the elements. It had been the gypsies and travellers' way of life for hundreds of years. But the Vagrancy Act of 1824 had made it an offence to sleep rough or beg, and people could be arrested and punished if considered to be doing this. If the men

179

couldn't show they had work, they would be classed as vagrants.

Just over a month after being married, with a child probably on the way, Thomas was likely to have been travelling, looking for work so that he could feed his family. Just camping in a field, making a temporary home. And what does he get? Two months in prison! Accused and convicted of *"threatening to invade the hedges and hen roosts of the neighbouring farmers"*! No evidence of the men doing this at all – just convicted for their very existence. Gypsies and Travellers had been persecuted for many years, and this was just a typical example of the use of the 1824 Vagrancy Act to get rid of men whose only crime was to be born poor.

OK, I've been on my soap box too long. I hope you understand why I was upset. The social injustice had really hit home. Interestingly, the 1861 census shows Thomas and Martha living in a tent with two children, Ann and John; along with his brother, Hugh, and his wife, Jane and children, Ann and Sarah. The address is "Rowan Tree" – probably the closest tree to the tent. Giving an address like this was common at the time, since it referred to a fixed spot, just as living in a house would. This time, they can avoid arrest under the Vagrancy Act, as Thomas and Hugh both give their occupations as "Basket Makers".

My next discovery of an arrest for Thomas sounds like it was for an early drink-driving offence. Although the headline sounds more like road rage. Reported in the Cumberland and Westmorland Advertiser, the story goes:

Westmorland Advertiser 15th September 1863

Alleged Furious Driving

Thomas Berry, basket maker, Penrith, was charged with furiously driving his horse and cart along the highway between Town End and the Vicarage, Penrith, on Thursday last.

The prisoner, hearing the charge read over, said, "I was driving a cart on the road; I had good leather reins to the horse; there was a man on a pony before me; some dogs jumped out and the pony fell over them."

Miss Elizabeth Whittington, Carleton Hall, said - on Thursday the 10th September, I was on the highroad between Penrith and the Vicarage. I saw a cart on the road. I was 100 yds from it. I heard it coming before it passed me. There was a man in the cart. The horse was coming very fast, as if the man had lost the control of it. I turned from the road to the footpath. The cart was not going so fast as it passed me. There was a man on horseback, galloping before it. The horse he was riding upon fell down, and the man in the cart drove over it. No person was hurt; but a dog was hurt by the horse on which the man rode. The horse in the cart was being driven beyond the proper speed. I was not afraid of being run over. It appeared that the man on horseback and the man in the cart were racing. As far as I could judge, the men were not quite sober.

The prisoner declined asking the witness any questions. He said "I have nothing to say, only that I was not going extra fast; I had no drink; I was on my own side of the road; the women in the cart were talking loud and fast; and the woman on the road would hear the cart a long time before I came up, and fancy it was going faster than it was.

Major Brougham, addressing the prisoner said: "According to the act of Parliament, you are liable to be fined £10, but as the witness has not said you were in liquor, you will only be fined 5s., and let this be a caution to you.

A narrow escape with a fine, this time.

By 1871, Thomas appears to be changing his ways to something like a settled life. He is living at Forster Street, Penrith, with his wife and five children, and his occupation is "Hawker." My guess is that, by now, the family stayed at the same place – "settled" – and Thomas travelled daily around a regular route, selling his baskets and possibly other items such as besoms and brooms at local markets, fairs and shops.

They might have stopped travelling and were settled, but they still lived in a gypsy/traveller community. I noticed that Thomas's neighbours had the familiar family names of Miller and Lowther, both very well-known Traveller family names – families that were very intertwined with the Berry's.

Apart from a couple of incidents when Thomas was fined a few shillings for allowing his horses to stray on public highways, I found no other serious convictions. It looks like a typical case of someone growing up and becoming sensible and law-abiding.

Considering his life and background, and his family's track-record, his brushes with the law were very minor. He lost his father – first to prison and transportation, then to death – when he was only a few years old. As the man of the house, he had to work from an extremely young age just to make ends meet. Then, marrying Martha and having a bunch of children to look after, he seemed to have been doing the best he could. My 3-times great grandfather had certainly gained my respect.

The next two censuses, of 1881 and 1891, show him still working as a hawker. On 19th May, 1892, Thomas, Martha and three of their children: Isabella, Joseph and Charles, emigrated to America onboard the RMS *Etruria*. The cost of a steerage ticket was around £50.00 each. Thomas must have been working hard and doing well, to have been able to save this amount of money. They had transported themselves to a new country, in search of a better life. The family passed through Ellis Island fifteen days later. Thomas's immigration papers show his occupation as "Horse Dealer."

Thomas Berry passed away on November 3rd 1897 at Benton, Columbia, Pennsylvania. His wife Martha returned to England sometime around the end of 1900 or early 1901. She is shown on the 1901 census living with family in Workington, Cumberland. Family stories passed down say that she came back to marry a Mr Matthew Dewsnap. This anecdotal evidence is interesting as no-one knew who Matthew was until many years later when this research was carried out. They didn't marry, and Martha returned to America sailing from Liverpool to Philadelphia on April 10th 1901 onboard the S.S. Waesland. Martha died on September 1st 1902 at Clearfield County, Pennsylvania.

Chapter 24
1851 - Hugh Berry

Hugh Berry was Thomas's older brother. I guessed that if Thomas and his father, John, had been on the wrong side of the law from time to time, there was a high likelihood that Hugh had been, too. But first, I wanted to find him in the census, to pick up his basic details.

He appeared in 1851, living at Rawhead, near Penrith, lodging with Matthew Dewsnip, a basket maker, and his wife, Ann Dewsnip. They had a baby daughter, Ann Dewsnip, aged 2 months.

Hugh and another boy, Thomas Watson, who was also lodging there, gave their occupations as Basket Makers.

I found the first newspaper report on Hugh in the Kendal Mercury, dated 11th June 1853, when he was nineteen years old. The article read:

Kendal Mercury 11th June 1853

William Miller, a potter, was brought up in custody of Constable Pharoah, and on the information of A. Huddleston. Esq., of Hutton John, charged with a multitude of offences; to wit, illegal fishing, trespass, sabbath desecration, forcibly releasing some donkeys from the Pinfold, encamping in the open air, &c. &c. It appears, however, that Hugh Berry and Andrew Cummings, gentlemen of the same kidney as Miller, had taken a part in these misdemeanours. The case was adjourned till next sitting day, warrants in the meantime having been issued for the apprehension of the other two.

"Gentlemen of the same kidney!" That was an expression I'd never heard before! I Googled it to find its meaning, but never found a clear explanation. Basically, I think it just means "similar people".

I quickly found the report of the court case and found that only William Miller was indicted. Hugh and Andrew Cummins can't have been found, or there wasn't enough evidence to indict them. William got away with a 5 shilling fine.

I'd found Hugh's marriage when I was looking for Thomas's. He had also been married at Allison's Bank Toll House, to a Jane Lowther, on 31st March, 1855. Only three weeks after his marriage, however, Hugh was in trouble and was arrested on suspicion of stealing. Reading the report, I found one of the names of Hugh's accomplices interesting.

Westmorland Gazette 21st April 1855

Four men of the potter and tinker fraternity, who gave the names of Hugh Berry, John Duffy, Joseph Newlands and Matthew Parsnip.

Matthew Parsnip! Could this be the Matthew Dewsnip or Dewsnap that Hugh was lodging with, four years earlier? I had read that Travellers often gave officials false names that were very similar to their own. Particularly on census records, licenses, certificates, arrests etc. This was done to try to avoid accurate records being kept on them. The Travelling community had a great suspicion of authority. Could this be an example of that? 'I have a feeling it was also done tongue in cheek, making fun of authority. Hugh was held in gaol until the court case on 14th July.

Kendal Mercury 14th July 1855

Stealing Cart Covers

Hugh Berry, Basket-maker, age 20, neither reads nor writes, was indicted for stealing two woollen cart covers belonging to Mr. B. Eggleston, of Culgaith. The prisoner pleaded not guilty.

I won't transcribe the rest of the report. It's long and tedious and holds nothing more of interest. It just goes on to say that Hugh was found guilty and sentenced to two months' hard labour.

So, married on 31st March, arrested: 21st April, convicted: 14th July and released: 14th September. On October 13th, we already know from Thomas's convictions that they were both gaoled for two months – so they would have been released in mid-December. What a great start to their married life!

In the next interesting newspaper report I found, Hugh was in trouble, once again, with Matthew Dewsnip/Dewsnap/Parsnip. Here, called Tueslip.

RIOTOUS AND INDECENT BEHAVIOUR

Matthew Tueslip and Hugh Berry, potters living at Penrith, were brought before Col. Harrison and T Scott Esq. at the police court, on Friday last, charged with being drunk and guilty of riotous behaviour at Longwathby, on the previous afternoon, whereby they forfeited a sum of 40s each. P.C. Boan said he was called out to the prisoners about four o'clock, and found them very drunk, upon the public street, creating a disturbance, cursing and swearing, and using bad language. Berry had his coat off, and was wanting to fight a man near him. Their conduct was so violent that he was obliged to take then into custody. Berry was fined 7s and Tueslip 5s. The costs 8s, to be paid between them; and in default to be imprisoned in Carlisle gaol, seven days.

Drunk and disorderly. And once again, we have a great example of Matthew taking the mick out of authority by using an alias very similar to his real name. The big question is: what was his real name?

I traced his records and found that he was actually baptised as "Snapdew". But I've found him as Dewsnip, Dewsnop, Dewsnap, Dowsnop and Parsnip – as well as my latest find, Tueslip. I wonder if he invented that name because he was arrested on the Tuesday?

I know one should never judge, because we didn't live in those times; but we can't help having thoughts and opinions.

Thomas and Hugh must have had an appalling lifestyle – one that is almost impossible to comprehend, by our standards, today. Would they have got themselves into all this minor offending if their father, the main provider hadn't been transported? Did they offend just to feed their families and themselves? I can't help but feel a dreadful sadness for these people who are my family.

This feeling was compounded when I read the story of "The Penrith Bug Hole". The nickname it was given should give a decent enough clue about the living conditions in this residential area in Penrith.

Different newspapers described the place in different ways, but all of them are similar and they all contribute to building a clear mental image.

PUBLIC NOTICE.

WHEREAS

Divers complaints have been made to the MAGISTRATES of LEATH WARD, of Public Inconvenience experienced by the Inhabitants of the said Ward, from travelling

Potters, Tinkers, & Gipsies,

who encamp by the Road Side, turn their Cattle loose on the Highways, destroy the Fences, and commit various other depredations.

NOTICE IS HEREBY GIVEN,

That the High Constable has received Special Orders to Apprehend and bring before the Magistrates, all persons guilty of such Unlawful Practices, and further, TO REQUIRE ALL THE LOCAL CONSTABLES AND SURVEYORS OF HIGHWAYS, to aid in preventing such Nuisances within their respective limits, and in bringing the offending parties to Punishment; and they are hereby further required to take Notice, that if it shall be proved that any Neglect of Duty shall have taken place by any of the said Officers, in relation thereto, proceedings will be taken against them to enforce the Penalties thereby incurred.

By order,

M. SCOTT, High Constable.

☞ The Surveyors are requested to Post this up in some Public Place in their Township immediately, and to call for more at the Magistrates' Office next time they are in Penrith.

They are expected to pay particular attention to the Orders herein; if not, the Penalties will be strictly enforced.

Penrith, 23rd March, 1852.

H. BROWN, PRINTER, PENRITH.

Gypsy Poster
186

Carlisle Journal 31st December 1867

The building adjacent to the new market house was occupied by wretched hovels, the abodes of the poor, and places where all kinds of vice, crime and disease were nurtured. Adjoining the new market house stands a filthy block of buildings, known by the very appropriate title of Bug Hole. This place is tenanted, in those parts where shelter can be obtained, chiefly by loose women and what are called Travellers and the place appears to take its name from a species of Traveller who do not travel far beyond its precincts…

…a place which is a nuisance, and a den of vice and disease, and a standing disgrace to the town in which it stands.

So, you might ask: what does this have to do with the Berrys? Well, in 1865, Hugh lived there. In his own words:

Cumberland & Westmorland Advertiser 1st August 1865

I live in Bug Hole, and occupy one room. It is 7ft. 6in. high, 16ft. long and 10ft. wide. It is upstairs. Myself, my wife, and four children live there. Three of the children are now in the small-pox, and one has just got better. I pay my rent to Robert Howe, and have done for twelve months. I took the room from Howe, and I pay him 1s a week rent. I did not look for another house, it is good enough for me, or any other poor man.

Hugh was giving evidence in a survey which had been served on the owners and occupiers of "Bug Hole" by the Penrith Board of Guardians, after an order for improvements had been made by the Highway Committee.

What choice did Hugh have? He could camp in the clean, fresh air and be persecuted and gaoled as a rogue and vagabond, or live in the Bug Hole, in filth and deprivation. This isn't a made-up story: it was real life. And the worst part is yet to come. Just a few months after Hugh said, "it is good enough for me," his 2 year-old daughter, Margaret, died.

This extract from Benjamin Disraeli's novel *Sybil*, published in 1845, goes to the heart of one of the most controversial subjects of 19th century history – the extent to which industrialisation improved or depressed living standards, and the ways in which the poor were treated.

Two nations between whom there is no intercourse and no sympathy; who are ignorant of each other's habits, thoughts and feelings, as if they were dwellers in different zones or inhabitants of different planets; who are formed by different breeding, are fed by different food, are ordered by different manners, and are not governed by the same laws ... THE RICH AND THE POOR.

By 1871, Hugh and Jane Berry had five children and were living at Brown's Yard, Scotland Road. The census in 1881 saw him still in Scotland Road, but now at No. 74, and with seven children.

Something was clearly happening in Hugh's life. I suspect the responsibility of family life was pushing him to work harder and smarter in his basket making business. On 11th February 1888, Hugh took part in the Penrith Art and Industrial Exhibition, entering his swills (traditional baskets) in the Basket and Rush work section. He was awarded second place.

By the time of the 1891 census, the family had only moved two doors away to No. 76, and now Hugh describes himself as a "Swill Maker". This was a step up from a common basket maker, since Cumberland swills were a much more substantial type of basket. Made from strips of coppiced oak, swills were still woven, whereas trugs, which looked similar, were nailed together. Swills were much preferred for heavy agricultural or industrial use.

It looks as if Hugh was slowly dragging his family's living standards in the right direction.

Hugh had one or two very minor offences from the mid '60s onwards, but nothing serious. By the time of the 1901 census, he is shown as living in Egremont, West Cumberland, although I don't know exactly when he moved there. He probably went to live in that area because there was more industry, and a greater chance to improve his lot. He died in 1904.

IMPRESSIVE FUNERAL AT
EGREMONT

Yesterday (Friday) afternoon the funeral of Mr Hugh Berry, of Church Street, Egremont took place at the cemetery, Egremont, the burial service being conducted by the Rev. W. Thwaites. The coffin was covered with floral tokens of respect for the dead. Mr Berry and his wife - who predeceased him by about nine months - hawked in the district of Egremont for many years with earthenware, and they were very much respected owing to their kindly dispositions. A considerable number of relatives and friends followed the remains to their resting place. There were four generations represented at the funeral including the deceased's father, who must be about 90 years of age, and who had walked 17 miles in the fell district in order to get a train to reach Egremont. Deceased was 70 years of age. Prolonged regret is felt by his friends at his death, and perhaps no funeral in the town has been characterised by more reverence than that of Mr Berry. Like his wife, the deceased was a victim to cancer. He was a native of Penrith and followed his trade all his life.

We know from research that the person mentioned as Hugh's father is actually his step-father; since Hugh's genetic father, John Berry, had been transported in 1839. For this very old man, to walk 17 miles to attend Hugh's funeral just shows how close the family were.

From abject poverty, to being successful and respected. Good on you, Hugh!

A year later, it was reported:

IN MEMORIAM

Berry. - In loving memory of our dear father and mother, Hugh and Jane Berry, who died in Egremont, November 28th 1903 and August 9th 1904, formerly of Penrith.

Taken aside by Jesus
To feel the touch of his hand
To rest for a while in the shadow
Of the rock in the weary land.

They miss them most who loved them best.
Ever remembered by their sons and daughter.
C, J and M Berry.

John Berry's first-born daughter, Jane, was baptised in 1830. There were no requirements for people with no fixed abode, such as Gypsies and Travellers, to take part in the 1841 census. This was probably the reason I could find no reference to her there. Much later I found two references, one in John's court case the other in his transportation records, stating the he had two children. This referred to his sons Hugh and Thomas, so unfortunately Jane must have died. The second daughter, Mary, was baptised in 1831 at St Mary's Church, Carlisle. Sadly, I found her burial recorded a little over a year later in 1832, at Brampton, just outside Carlisle.

The final child for me to search for was Ann. She was the daughter who was born after her father was sent to be transported. I found her baptism at Torpenhow, the same place as most of her siblings. She was recorded as: "Ann, daughter of John and Ann Berry." Her father's occupation was "Besom Maker," the same as on the other children's baptism records.

Making besoms (hazel-twig brooms) and making baskets went hand-in-hand, and John was described variously as a maker of each, on different documents. Finding anything else on Ann was proving difficult. Again, I thought perhaps she'd married and changed her name, until I came across the death of an Ann Berry in 1848. The name fitted, but it was a fairly common name. The place of death, Unthank, was in the region her parents travelled through – which was promising. So, I took a chance and ordered the death certificate. When it arrived, it was all there:

> *died 28th May 1848, Ann Berry, 9 years old, Daughter of John Berry, Basket Maker, (deceased), cause of death, Croup, 30 Hours. William Carrick in attendance.*

What a shame. To die so young, and of something so simple as croup, so easily cured these days. I never found who William Carrick, the person present at her death, was. Perhaps he had adopted her, or maybe he was a close family friend – but maybe something will crop up in the future that will shed some light.

So, that was it. At that point, I'd traced all John Berry's children as best I could, but still had absolutely nothing on his wife, Ann. I'd searched every database, parish register, Bishop's transcript and census records – and just drawn a blank. That's when my DNA test proved to be invaluable.

Chapter 25
1839 - Hutchinson's and Berry's

DNA was becoming a popular addition to conventional genealogy research. After a slow and expensive beginning, it was now more affordable, and enough people had tested to make a worthwhile database for matching samples.

I tested my DNA with a commercial genealogical company, who provide an autosomal test that can be linked to your family tree on their website. This means that anyone else on their database whose DNA matched yours would be highlighted. You can then try to work out where your family trees cross.

It took about 4 weeks from sending my sample to the company, to seeing the results appear on their website. The first report, on my ethnicity, told me about my genetic background and where my ancestors came from. It was interesting, but it wasn't the reason I had taken the test. For my own purposes, what I really wanted to see were the people I was genetically matched with.

I turned eagerly to these results and read the list of genetic matches. At first, I was a bit overwhelmed with the sheer number of matches I had. Hundreds! Of course, I had no idea where they connected to me on my tree. Were they matches on my maternal or paternal sides? My father's maternal or paternal sides? My mother's maternal or paternal? And so on. Some fractions of shared chromosomes were so minimal, my relationship to them was impossibly distant.

The only way to start was from the beginning. The first half-dozen or so matches, I already knew – family members and extended family – people I already had linked up to, in my tree. Then, it got interesting.

I went back to the first unknown match, listed as M.L. (managed by pauldlovell). I'd never heard of him!

The match gave me possible relationship range somewhere between 3rd - 4th cousin with an "extremely high" confidence level of it being a correct match. Uploading my DNA to another genealogical website , I learned that we matched on chromosomes 3 and 13 with a total match of 64.5 centimorgans. This gave an estimated MRCA (Most Recent Common Ancestor) of 3.9 generations. It all looked very interesting, but to be perfectly honest, in those days, I didn't have a clue what it all meant.

Next, I clicked on the "View Match" button, and this gave me access to his tree. It also told me the family names we had in common: Knowles and

Berry. I recognised both of those immediately.

Looking at his tree, I saw individual names I recognised, but I still couldn't see the place where our families merged. The website gives the option of sending a message to your match, so I did that immediately. Paul replied the same day, and after several messages back and forth, we worked out that his great grandmother, Martha Knowles, and my great grandmother, Annie Knowles, were sisters.

Martha was born in 1883. She wasn't shown as being with the family on the 1891 census because she was staying with Thomas and Martha Berry, her grandparents. By the time of the 1901 census, she had married Jacob Miller (marrying into another large Travelling family who's surname crops up continually throughout this story)), so she was, by then, Martha Miller. You can see how easily I'd missed her, and without DNA I would never have made the connection.

Since Martha was a direct ancestor of Paul's, he had invested in buying birth and marriage certificates, this gave him full provenance. So, that was my first DNA match sorted. Paul and I were 3rd cousins, sharing one set of great great grandparents, Richard Knowles and Annie Berry.

Having access to Paul's tree, I had a quick look around, just out of interest. It only took moments to spot something very interesting. As I mentioned, Martha Knowles married Jacob Miller. His parents were George Miller and Mary Ann Dewsnap. Now, that name rang a very big bell – or more like a gong. Dewsnap, Dewsnip, Parsnip – could there be a connection?

Sure enough, Mary Ann Dewsnap's parents were the same Matthew and Ann Dewsnip that Hugh Berry had been lodging with, at the time of the 1851 census.

This meant that I had to do some deeper Dewsnap digging – and sooner rather than later. I got cracking, straight away. Matthew and Ann had two children, Mary Ann and another Matthew (let's call him Matthew 2).

Matthew 2 married Margaret Hamilton and had a bunch of children. One of these was a son, Thomas. Going down Thomas's branch, I eventually came to his grandson, Steve Vickers. With a bit of detective work using the genealogical site I subscribed to, I was able to make contact with Steve.

As luck had it, Steve was also seriously interested in family history and shared with me all the information he'd gathered on the Dewsnap's. Amongst the copies of certificates he sent me was Matthew 2's death certificate. Scottish death certificates feature the names of the deceased's parents and their occupations. This was very interesting.

As expected, Matthew 2's father was Matthew Dewsnap, Basket Maker (deceased).

Then, my eyes widened in surprise. His mother was "Ann Dewsnap, previously Berry, M.S. (Maiden Surname) Hutchinson (deceased)."

It took a few minutes for this to register. Slowly the fog lifted from my brain, and I began to see the implications of this snippet of information, which became one of the most significant links in my genealogical chain.

She was Ann Berry! Who had been Hutchinson! The mystery of what had happened to John Berry's wife was solved in an instant. It had been staring me in the face all the time. I just hadn't seen it.

After her husband John Berry's demise, Ann had married Matthew Dewsnap. Later searches of marriages at Allisons Bank Toll House at Gretna, showed me that they'd married on 30th March 1850.

A small but important piece of the jigsaw was on Matthew 2's baptism record, where his mother is shown as "Mary Ann Dewsnap". She must have gone by her middle name, Ann, for much of her life. The relevance of her full name, Mary Ann, comes later.

Now, the pieces were slotting together, and it all began to make sense. In 1851, the young Hugh Berry had been actually living with his mother – he was not simply a lodger. All those times he got into trouble with Matthew Dewsnap/Dewsnip/Tueslip/Parsnip – that was his stepfather!

Matthew Dewsnap was the old man who had walked 17 miles to Hugh's funeral in 1904. The jigsaw puzzle was finally coming together and the picture becoming much clearer.

Mathew Dewsnap's Death Certificate

Chapter 26
Piecing Things Together

I went back through the family tree to explore further, wondering what had happened with the Berry family in those lost years. I hoped I could continue unravelling the connections with Ann or Mary Ann, and get some more clarity on the complex family relationships I was uncovering.

I went to John Berry's father, whose details I had only skimmed up to now.

John Berry's parents were Charles and Christiana Berry. The first reference I'd found that mentioned John's parents was the report of his father's response to John's conviction in 1838.

Westmorland Gazette 13th August 1838

"His father gave vent to his feelings in loud and agonised cries of grief".

The second reference was on a letter from John's friend, when he was begging for clemency for John, also in 1838:

"He has a wife and two children in great distress and his father is a blind man depending partly on him for his support."

So, Charles was blind, and was dependent on John, to a degree. I wondered what had happened to him after losing his son to transportation.

But first, what kind of a man was John Berry's father? Was he something of a rogue, too? I presumed his eyes had failed, with age. Maybe poor eyesight didn't hinder criminal activity.

A search for offences by Berry's in Cumbria archive records of petty sessions revealed that, on 26th September, 1816, Charles Berry, a coal carrier and potter, was fined five shillings for being drunk.

The following year, 1817, the Carlisle Patriot reported on 10th May that four men, including Charles Berry, had broken into Matthew Blackstock's mill and stolen 50 stone (320kg) of oatmeal and four sacks. The story reported clearly shows it was Charles Berry's horse and cart that were used.

The Berry's, Hutchinson's and Gregg's were proving to be well matched family groups. Charles and two of his accomplices had managed to avoid arrest and on 31st May and 7th June, an advert was published in the Patriot.

A Reward of FIVE GUINEAS for each will be paid to any Person who shall lodge the whole or either of them in any of his Majesty's Gaols in England or Scotland on application to the CLERK OF THE PEACE, CARLISLE.

The size of the reward clearly indicates that this was considered to be a serious felony.

From the reward advertisement, we have a short description of Charles:

About 32 years of age, 5 feet 3 inches high. Very swarthy complexion, and very shabbily dressed.

It also states: "used to work with Horses and Carts."

Then, the years slide away, with no reports of Charles committing any crimes (or being caught) – until 1838, when, just over half a year before his son John was charged, the Northern Liberator reported:

Northern Liberator 6th January 1838

JAMES OSMOTHER and CHARLES BURY were charged with passing base coin, at Hexham Fair, on 8th November. Mr. Ingham stated the case. It appeared that Charles Bury, who was blind, gave the other prisoner, a boy, a base sixpence, who paid it to Mrs. Davison for some bread. Bury was then recognised as having before offended in the same way, and was taken into custody and searched, and there was good money found upon him, both in silver and copper, and in a secret pocket, 53 bad shillings and 34 bad sixpences. Verdict, Guilty. To be imprisoned and kept to hard labour for six calendar months.

So, sometime between 1817 and 1838, Charles had lost his sight. I suppose we'll never know how. A picture of Charles is developing. The Northern Liberator article stated that "Bury was recognised as having before offended in the same way."

So, Charles was an habitual offender. Perhaps specialising in passing counterfeit coins.

I'm speculating that Charles hid behind his blindness. If he was caught, he could say that, with him being blind, he had no idea: he must have recently accepted the counterfeit money without seeing that it was bad.

So, regardless of any excuse, Charles was convicted on January 6th and sentenced to six months, with hard labour. A quick calculation works out that he would have been released on or just before 6th July.

Passing base coins must have been very easy, very lucrative, or maybe both. Or perhaps Charles was so desperate to earn money, maybe due to his disability, that almost immediately after being released from gaol, he was at it again.

On 13th July, the following article was printed in the Carlisle Journal. Everyone was in it!

Carlisle Journal 13th July 1839

COUNTERFEIT COINS - On Saturday evening last, Haugh, one of our police officers, received information that a person was attempting to pass a counterfeit shilling at the shop of Mr. Wyllie, flax dresser, in this city, and on going there he observed a woman named Christiana Berry, a "smasher" of no mean pretensions, leaving the shop. He watched till she joined her daughter-in-law, Ann Berry, at the end of Saint Cuthbert's Lane about 20 yards from Mr. W.'s shop, and who had apparently been waiting to learn the "result" of her "guid" mother's mission. The suspicions of the officer became more excited on observing the "reinforcement," and he "kept an eye" on the parties till they adjourned to Head's Lane, a retired part of the town, to hold a "confab." This he unceremoniously stopped by taking them both into custody, and conveying them to the police office. On their way there, Christiana seemed very anxious about something which she had in her right-hand pocket, but the officer prudently compelling them to walk before him, prevented her from quitting the "tin", and on her being searched at the office three counterfeit shillings and a counterfeit sixpence were found in the self-same pocket. Haugh and Kent, another police officer, were then dispatched by the superintendent to the house of Charlie Berry, a well-known "banker", and the husband of Christiana, with instructions to search for the "specie". On arriving there, "Charlie" was in the act of consigning himself to the arms of "nature's sweet restorer", but, upon being acquainted with the object of the officers' visit, he became very anxious to possess himself of his. "oh no, we never mention them," which Kent, perceiving, prevented him, and on searching the pockets, found a couple of counterfeit sixpences; on further search, the officers found 84 counterfeit shillings, and 56 counterfeit sixpences, the principal part concealed in the chimney. Charlie, of course, was taken to comfort his "better-half" in durance. The officers were then dispatched to Torpenhow, to look after Nanny Hutchinson, the mother of Ann Berry, who had been seen by the police on that day, in Carlisle, "upon business". They arrived there about three on the Sunday morning, and on obtaining admittance commenced their search. Nanny was prodigiously anxious to obtain possession of her pockets; this did not escape the notice of the officers, who "got first hold," and on examination they were found to contain 16 counterfeit shillings, three counterfeit sixpences, two pounds six shillings and sixpence in good money, and a ticket purporting that she was in the receipt of parochial relief from the parish of Seaton! The parties were examined and committed to prison by T. C. Heysham, Esq., mayor, on Monday last. Charlie is a blind man, and has been in "trouble" before.

Welcome to my family, my 5-times great grandparents, Charles and Christiana Berry, in all their glory.

There was my 4-times great grandmother, Ann Berry, wife of John Berry who was in gaol waiting trial for stabbing his friend (and future wife of Matthew Dewsnap). There, too, was Ann (Nanny) Hutchinson, mother of Ann Berry, nee Hutchinson – my 5 times Great Grandmother. What a bunch of scallywags.

I was still pursuing Charles through the documentation, and trying to piece his life together. It was said that Charles had "been in trouble before." I knew of a couple of instances, but I wondered how many more there were.

Charles was referred to in the newspaper article as a "Banker" – someone known to clip gold and silver coins, melt down the metal clippings and sell it on. Christiana was described as a "Smasher" – someone who passed counterfeit coins. Banker and Smasher – what a double-act. They must have been very well-known in Carlisle to have been awarded these fine titles.

I think a fair guess is that when Charles was caught at Hexham, he was already in possession of all the coins, having thought that by using his family to distribute them, they could be passed on in Carlisle.

The most coincidental thing of all was that Christiana and Ann were first spotted together in St Cuthbert's Lane, and then followed and apprehended in Heads Lane. These are the sites of my two favourite coffee shops in Carlisle – and somewhere I visit several times each week. I'd been walking in their footsteps for years without knowing it.

On 10th August, the local newspaper reported on the court case.

Carlisle Journal 10th August 1839

CHARLES BERRY (72)

charged with having in his possession one hundred pieces of false and counterfeit coin, resembling, and apparently intended to resemble and pass for shillings, and sixty pieces of false and counterfeit coin, resembling, and apparently intended to resemble and pass for sixpences, with intent unlawfully to utter the same.

Mr. Armstrong and Mr. Fawcett conducted the case for the prosecution, and Mr. Ramshay appeared for the prisoner.

Joseph Haugh (by Mr. Fawcett) — I am a police officer in Carlisle. I know the prisoner. He has a house in Ritson's Lane, in this city. He has lived there better than nine months. On the night of the 6th of July, at twenty minutes to ten o'clock, I went with Kent, another police officer, to search the house of the prisoner. Berry was at home, and an old man was sitting with him. I told him we had come to search his house for bad money. He said we might search. He was undressed, as if going into bed. I saw him as if wishing to get hold of his breeches. He got hold of them, and Kent took them from him. Kent searched his breeches. We searched the house, and Kent found a tea-pot in a cupboard behind the bed. I looked up the chimney, and saw a brick standing out. It was about as high as I could reach. I took the brick out, and behind it was a tin box. I took it out, and found in it 103 shillings and 60 sixpences. I have had it in my possession ever since. No one else lived in the house, that I am aware of, except Berry and his wife. They have only one room.

By Mr. Ramshay — I know Berry and his wife. I will not swear that no person lives with them. An old man was sitting behind the door when I went in. I saw only one bed. As soon as we told him what we wanted he tried to get his breeches. I will swear that they were off — that he was placing them on a chair when he went in. He did not prevent us searching.

By Mr. Armstrong — When we went in Berry was sitting on the bed. His breeches were on the chair back. He made for them immediately. He grappled for them.

John Kent — (by Mr. Armstrong)— I am a police officer. I went with Joseph Haugh to search the prisoner's house. An old woman was sitting with him when we went in. Berry's breeches were then under the bolster, and he appeared himself to be getting off the bed. At the time we went in there was no light; we inquired for a candle, and procured a light from the next door neighbour. When we told him we had come to search for counterfeit coin, he said we were welcome to do so. In a cupboard behind the bed we found a teapot containing sixteen sixpences and shillings. There was a box behind the bed. I said to Haugh, "It is locked." The prisoner said the key was in his breeches. He made to the bed and got hold of them. His back was towards me. I asked him what he was doing, and took the trousers from him. In one pocket I found two sixpences, but there was no key. We found one sixpence on a shelf.

By Mr. Ramshay — I have known Berry to have lived there these twelve months. I saw him in this house last winter.

By the Judge — I here produce all the money that was found.

Haugh recalled by his Lordship — I found no good money in the House. I brought all the bad away.

William Hayton — (By Mr. Fawcett)— I live at Orton. The prisoner rents a house off me. He has occupied it twelve or fourteen months.

By Mr. Ramshay — I have called to see him sometimes. He is a middling good tenant. I have worse. He paid me one shilling weekly. He is a little in arrears. He never paid me with bad money. His wife used to work for me. I have known her a long time.

John Brown — I am a silversmith in Carlisle. The money now shown to me is bad. His Lordship requested Mr. Brown to examine every sixpence and shilling separately. He did so and said they were every one bad. They were all of the same kind of metal.

Mr. Ramshay addressed the Jury at considerable length in defence of the prisoner.

His Lordship summed up the evidence, and the Jury, after retiring for about a quarter of an hour, gave in a verdict of Guilty.

Sentence — To be imprisoned two years, and to be kept to hard labour.

ANN HUTCHINSON, (75) charged with having in her possession sixteen pieces of false and counterfeit coins resembling and apparently intended to resemble and pass for sixpences, well knowing the same to be false and counterfeit, and with intent unlawfully to utter the same.

Mr. Armstrong and Mr. Fawcett conducted the case for the prosecution, and Mr. Ramshay appeared for the prisoner.

Joseph Haugh (by Mr. Fawcett) - I went on 7th of July to search the prisoner's house, at Torpenhow. I found her at home, but in bed. She came down stairs and let us in. Kent, another police officer, went with me. We said we were come to search the house for bad money, and she said we might search. She then went upstairs, and Kent followed her. When she got upstairs she ran to the bed-side, and took hold of her pockets. Kent said I must see first what is in them, and took them from her. She said there was something in which she wanted out, as it belonged to another person. Kent searched her pockets, and found in it two shillings and sixteen sixpences of bad money; and £2 6s 6d. in silver of good money. The bad money was kept separate from the good. There was fivepence of copper loose in her pocket.

By Mr. Ramshay - We knocked at her door, and waited five minutes before she let us in. She asked, "Who's there?" We said it is us. Do not know that she was aware that we were constables. The prisoner keeps a lodging-house. She said the money wasn't hers.

John Kent (by Mr. Armstrong) - I went with Haugh to search the house of the prisoner. She was undressed when she let us in. She went upstairs, and I followed her. She got hold of her pockets, and I took them from her. I said I must see what is in them. I found some bad money. She said a woman in Carlisle had given it to her, and she was rather dubious it was not good. There were two shillings and sixteen sixpences. She also had £2 6s 6d. of good money, kept separate from the bad. The whole was folded up in a gown sleeve.

By Mr. Ramshay - She had no purse. The gown sleeve answered the purpose of a purse. She said she had suspicion the money was not good, but it was given to her by a woman in Carlisle.

Mr. Brown, silversmith, examined the money as in the last case, and pronounced it to be all bad.

Mr. Ramshay addressed the Jury on behalf of the prisoner.

His Lordship summed up the evidence, and the Jury retired. They shortly afterwards returned with a verdict of Guilty.

Sentence - To be imprisoned twelve calendar months, and to be kept to hard labour.

CHRISTIANA BERRY (50) charged with having in her possession three pieces of false and counterfeit coins, resembling, and apparently intended to resemble and pass for shillings, knowing the same to be false and counterfeit, with intent unlawfully to utter the same.

Mr. Armstrong and Mr. Fawcett conducted the case for the prosecution. The prisoner in this case was not defended.

Sarah Wylie (by Mr. Fawcett) - My mother keeps a shop in Carlisle. On the 6th of July, between eight and nine o'clock in the evening, the prisoner came to buy a paper of pins. My mother, Mrs. Brown, and a young man who formerly lived with us, and myself were in the shop. I called for my mother to serve the prisoner with the pins. She gave my mother a shilling. My mother thought it was a bad one, and gave it to me to look at. I said it is a bad one. The prisoner said, "Let me have it again, and I will try it with some flint I have in my pocket." I asked her to let me see it again, and I showed it to the young man standing by, and he gave it back to the prisoner. She then left the shop.

Sarah Brown - I was in Mrs. Wylie's shop on the 6th of July when the prisoner came in. She wanted some pins and gave a shilling to pay for them. The shilling proved to be a bad one. I did not have it in my hand but I saw it. I left the prisoner in the shop. I saw Haugh the police officer standing outside of the door when I went out, and soon after saw the prisoner in his custody.

His Lordship asked the prisoner if she wished to put any questions to Mrs. Brown - She said she had none to put to her - Mrs. Brown was a rich woman and she was a poor one, and therefore nothing that she could say would be of any use.

Joseph Waugh - On the 6th July I saw the prisoner come out of Mrs. Wylie's shop. I followed her to Heads Lane. She was then in company with another woman who had joined her at St Cuthbert's Lane end. I saw they took notice of me and went up to them. I asked her how she came to offer a bad shilling? She said she had not one, and I took them both to the police office. When at the police office I observed her to be passing something from her right hand to her left. She stood with her left side to the fire. Kent seized her hand and he and I took 3s. 6d. from her, which I now produce. She was searched and 3d. of copper was found in a small box.

John Kent - I was in the police office when the prisoner was brought in. I assisted Haugh in taking something from her; it was 3s. 6d., which she was passing from one hand to the other. The money was bad.

Mr. Brown was called again, and examined the money as before. He said it was all bad.

The prisoner said it was the first time she had been guilty of any crime and begged for mercy.

His Lordship summed up the evidence and the Jury returned a verdict of Guilty.

Sentence - To be imprisoned six months, and to be kept to hard labour.

What a gang! The descriptions in these reports was so graphic, I could just imagine the scene in the dark, crowded house, as they tried to conceal their guilt during the raid by the constables; Charles with his britches off, ready for bed. The scene in the shop, Christiana denying everything. Innocents, all – according to themselves. But the evidence was incontrovertible.

Ann Berry, who was mentioned in the first newspaper report, was not indicted. My guess is that she had no "bad money" in her possession and therefore was not charged.

The sentences were clearly proportionate to the number of counterfeit coins each had in their possession, and not jointly as a gang. I wonder if they knew just how lucky they were to get a prison sentence with hard labour? Only two years earlier, Sir Robert Peel's government had introduced a bill to reduce the sentence for uttering counterfeit coin. Pre-1836, they could all have been sentenced to death.

Another very interesting point to note, is that Officer John Kent, who is mentioned several times in the news report, was the first black police officer in the UK. The son of a freed slave, he joined the Carlisle force in 1825. His career ended when he was dismissed for being drunk on duty. John Kents story is well documented in Ray Greenhow's book "Britains first black policeman" which mentions the Berry's and Hutchinson's.

There are huge anomalies in the Berry's ages. If Charles was 72, he would have to have been born in 1767. The reward advertisement for apprehending him for robbing from the corn mill in 1817 gives his age as 32; therefore suggesting that he was born in 1785. The 1851 census later shows his age as 79, so he must have been born in 1772. And his death certificate in 1856 gives his age as 84, once again suggesting that he was born in 1772.

At first, this made me doubt that the mill robber was the same Charles. His description as a carter, as highlighted, was good circumstantial evidence. Searching for a birth five years each side of 1785 turned nothing up. Likewise, the 1841 and '51 censuses didn't show a Charles Berry who had been born anywhere close to 1785. My opinion is that this discrepancy is down to either a misprint in that news report (31 instead of 51) or the simple possibility is that it was just another case of a mistruth.

Christiana is reported to be 50, so would have been born in 1789. From the 1841 census, she must have been born in 1791 and the '51 census suggests 1787. Her death certificate also in 1851 gives her age as 73, so that would mean she had been born in 1778.

Taking into account that most people in these times could neither read nor write, could illiteracy be the cause for these differences? They wouldn't have kept records. Did they just forget or lose track? Did people actually know the year they were born?

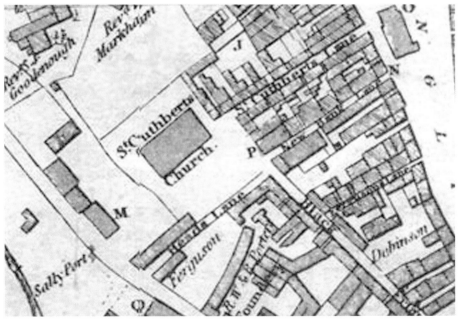

Map of Carlisle, showing St Cuthbert's Lane and Heads Lane

Whatever their ages, hard labour was exactly as described: hard. And it must have been extremely hard for a blind old man. They would have had to endure breaking stone for building roads, or picking oakum which would have been impossible for a blind man. Maybe they endured the treadmill, turning the crank or passing the shot, we'll never know for sure, but serve their time they did

Christiana was released after six months and can be found in the 1841 census, living in Carlisle with two lodgers. Charles is also on the 1841 census "in Carlisle gaol."

By the time of the 1851 census, Charles had been released and was living with Christiana in Wigton, together with eight lodgers. Christiana died the same year, on May 15th, and is probably buried in Wigton Cemetery. Charles went back to Carlisle, where he lived until 30th December, 1856. He now lies in a communal paupers' grave in Carlisle Cemetery.

Ann Berry went on to live what seems to be an uneventful life with Matthew Dewsnap, having two more children. She died on 14th July, 1883, and was laid to rest in a paupers' grave in St Michael's Church yard, Dalston, the village where I now live. Another amazing coincidence.

Chapter 27
1839 - Richard Hutchinson

Richard Hutchinson had always been an enigmatic character in my family tree. I had clear paper provenance proving that he was my 4-times great grandfather, but I couldn't get further back nor connect him to William Hutchinson, who I suspected hw was closely related to.

Richard's daughter, Martha Hutchinson, had married Thomas Berry, as I had already established.

And Thomas Berry's mother was Mary Ann Hutchinson, daughter of William Hutchinson and Ann Irvin.

But were Mary Ann Hutchinson and Richard Hutchinson related in some way? Even brother and sister?

My guess was that Richard's daughter, Martha and Mary-Ann's son, Thomas Berry, were first cousins – and they had married one another, since this type of marriage was not uncommon amongst Travelling people.

If that was the case, it meant that my DNA couldn't effectively be used for good comparisons, because I could have inherited certain DNA from either route, which complicated things.

My first reason for suspecting that Richard might be William Hutchinson's son came from his marriage record, which I found an Gretna Green, Blacksmith marriage records.

Page 153 of the marriage register, dated December 1832, reads:

Richard Hutchinson from the parish of Seaton in the County of Cumberland and Mary Allan from the parish of Westward in the County of Cumberland was married before the witnesses Richard Hutchinson and Mary Allan this twenty second day of December Eighteen hundred and thirty two years.

Richard's being from Seaton, the same village as William, gave me the first clue.

Checking the baptism records of Richard's children, I found that his occupation is shown as basket maker, besom maker or travelling potter. The 1851 census shows him living in a tent at "Teeside", County Durham, and again, his occupation is recorded as a basket maker. This all looked good, as far as my theory was concerned. It looked as if Richard was following the occupation of his father, but it still wasn't enough evidence. If I was to prove that William really was his father, it left another anomaly: there was no clue as to whether Ann Gregg or Ann Irving was his mother.

At times, researching family history is more like being a detective, following hunches or bringing back to memory details you've seen somewhere before. I remembered the newspaper report of John Berry's court case, where it was stated that John Berry was with Hutchinson, his brother-in-law, and Allan. Could this be the connection?

John Berry was married to Mary Ann Hutchinson; so, Richard could be her brother – which would make him John's brother-in-law, as the report had stated.

The name Allan also rang a bell. When William, Ann and family were arrested for stealing the 17 geese, there was a John Allan lodging at the house.

I was getting closer, but what finally convinced me that I was on the right track was the following:

Cumberland Paquet October 1st 1839

A man named Richard Irving, alias Hutchinson, a potter, was taken into custody at Hesket New Market on Thursday last, by Douglas the Cockermouth constable, after a two days' chase, for having in his possession a quantity of finished and unfinished base coin, in shilling and sixpenny pieces. He was taken before Mr. Dand, of Wigton on Friday, and fully committed to the House of Correction at Cockermouth, to take trial at the ensuing sessions. Two women belonging to this vendor of base coin, and no doubt participators in his illegal calling, are still at large.

This Richard was using at least one alias, but the two names Irving and Hutchinson were both highly relevant to me. This was very, very promising. Not to mention added coincidence of the counterfeit coin, family connection. However, It still didn't tell me who his mother was, so I was still clutching for straws..

This was followed a couple of weeks later by a newspaper report of the court case.

RICHARD IRVING (aged 22) was indicted for having in his possession eight shillings and ten sixpences of base coin, well knowing the same to be false and counterfeit.

The Prosecution was instituted by the Mint, and was conducted by Mr Fawcett and Mr Ramshay; and the prisoner was defended by Mr Bell.

Catherine Baty - My husband keeps an inn at Caldbeck. On the 25th September the prisoner came into our house, in company with Robert Jackson. He had a glass of rum. I over-heard him saying that the police were on the lookout for two women, who had been passing bad money. He said he knew how to make it, and could make it very well when he was sober, and had that on him which could make them. He said he had never passed any. I told this to my husband when he came, and he gave information to the Cockermouth constable.

By Mr Bell - The prisoner was a little fresh (tipsy).

Robert Jackson lives in Caldbeck. The conversation took place in the kitchen. I was in the bar.

Henry Douglas - I am a constable in Cockermouth. On the 25th and 26th September I was at Caldbeck, and on the latter day, I apprehended the prisoner at Hesket New Market. He was standing within the poor-house door, and I searched him immediately. He put his hand into his breeches pocket, and drew it out again immediately. I seized his hand, and found he had eight shillings and ten sixpences wrapped up in a piece of cloth. Two of the coins were finished; and the rest in the rough state.

By Mr Bell - The prisoner was very tipsy when I apprehended him.

George Graham - I am a watch maker. The coins produced are base metal - a compound of some kind.

Mr Bell addressed the Jury for the prisoner and called Richard Irving, who said he knew the prisoner. He had always borne a good character.

By Mr. Fawcett - He travels with pots. He was formerly a husbandman. He now lives in camps, by the hedge-sides.

The Jury immediately returned a verdict of guilty; and the court sentenced him to six months imprisonment, with hard labour. One week in solitary confinement.

This was really interesting. The first article refers to Richard as "Irving alias Hutchinson", the second, just as Irving. I have been fortunate enough to see original documents, showing the gaolers petition for payment in which he is referred to only as Irving. The court must have had clear proof that his correct name was Richard Irving.

I was getting warmer. It looked as if my suspicions were correct. And here was the likelihood that he was Ann Irving's son, rather than Ann Gregg's. If he was an Irving in his own right – he wasn't likely to be William Hutchinson's son, after all – or his legal name would have been Hutchinson.

I completely disregarded his age, because, so many times, I had found that such reports vary wildly from the truth.

Gaolers Petition for costs for Richard Irving

208

However, I think the final piece of strong circumstantial evidence came when I was comparing Richard's crime to another that followed only a few weeks later.

The second case involved people already mentioned in a previous chapter of "uttering base coin".

In both cases, the accused were passing counterfeit coins in a fairly small geographical area. Richard's case mentions two women "belonging to the vendor". These must have been his mother-in-law, Christiana Berry, and his sister, Mary Ann Berry, nee Hutchinson, who were involved in attempting to pass base coin Carlisle.

Finally, in the second case it was reported that after searching her house at Torpenhow, counterfeit coins were found at Nanny Hutchinson's house. Surely this was beyond coincidence?

To me, this was sufficient proof that Richard was Ann's son. However, for some reason, he had been named Irving, not Hutchinson. So, he must have been born before 1803, and was a brother to Elizabeth and Isabella Irving.

These three siblings had been born before Ann's relationship with William, so, Richard was not the son of William – and only a half-brother to George, Jane and Mary Ann Hutchinson.

Richard passed away on January 25th 1856 at Workington, Cumberland. His age shown on the death certificate is 57, making his year of birth 1799, which was after the days of Ann Gregg, but before the days of Ann Irvin. Who was Richard, Elizabeth and Isabella's father ?

Chapter 28
2018 - The Penny Finally Drops.

In the early part of my research, I was convinced that I was following the lives of several different women, all engaged in crimes of various types. It was like a flash of lightning when I decided to build a timeline. This narrowed things down to two possible culprits, eventually showing me that all these suspects were actually Ann Gregg, Just one person using many deceptions and aliases.

Another bolt of realisation came out of the blue now.

Ann Gregg disappeared sometime after her son, James, was baptised in 1801. Ann Irvin first appears on the scene at the baptism of her daughter Jane Hutchinson, at Camerton, in 1803.

There was no trace of Ann Gregg after 1801 – and no trace of Ann Irvin before 1803. Was it possible that they could they be the same person?

But if both Ann's *were* the same person, how did Richard, Isabella and Elizabeth Irving fit into the story? They would have been born during the time that Ann Gregg was in Giltspur Street Compter.

Could Ann have deliberately got pregnant in gaol to avoid transportation? I had read about this happening, but it was more anecdotal than proven. Could this be the proof that it actually happened?

If Richard, Isabella and Elizabeth were born in the compter, that would explain why they weren't called Hutchinson – but who was the father or fathers, and why the name Irving.

So many thoughts and ideas to try to unravel!

This is where DNA testing really came into its own. All I had to do was find descendants of Ann's children and get them to take an autosomal DNA test. That would allow me to compare the DNA of the descendants of one of Ann's children, with the DNA of descendants of another child. If I got matches, I would find answers.

If all my theorising was correct, Ann had thirteen children. Seven with William prior to her seven-year prison sentence; three in the compter, and a further three with William after being released.

What I needed to do was to split Ann's children into three groups, pre-1794,

1794 - 1801, and post- 1801 – and follow the lines of descent. This wasn't as daunting a task as it sounds, as having worked on my family tree for some time, I already knew some descendants in England who came down from Mary Ann Berry, nee Hutchinson. After John Berry's death, Mary Ann had married Matthew Dewsnap, and I was already in touch with four Dewsnap descendants, who had all taken autosomal tests.

My next line of thought was that George would be a good one to follow. He was transported in 1824, so there was no real chance that his descendants' DNA could be contaminated by cross-breeding with other relatives.

With Australia being a country full of immigrants, many family historians had taken DNA tests, looking to identify their ethnicity and family roots. This meant that it wasn't long before I had what I was looking for. I found a great great grand-daughter of George, whose DNA matched with all four of the other samples that I had matched!

What made this process all the more exciting was that all these people were my cousins, and all were interested in our wider family.

Provenance is vital when building a family tree. The more evidence on a relationship you have, the stronger the branches of your tree. I admit to being a bit pedantic with genealogy, so I decided to support my initial results by finding 1 or 2 more of George's descendants. This became so successful that not only did I have irrevocable evidence of the relationships, but I'd found so many cousins that we decided to form our own blog group on the internet, with everyone following this slowly unfolding story.

Making DNA comparisons isn't a difficult job. It's simply a case of getting everyone to upload their DNA to a specialist research website, which then compares the samples for you. This process looks for matching segments of DNA on a single chromosome, with a value greater than seven centimorgans.

I followed the same process, eventually tracing descendants of William and Peter Hutchinson from the first group of children; Isabella and Richard from the second group and George and Mary Ann from the third group.

By now, I had 40 to 50 DNA samples to cross-match. I had traced descendants to America, Canada, Mexico, Australia and New Zealand, as well as in the UK. Descendants in each group matched descendants in the other groups. I was correct in my assumption – and now, I had 100% proof.

Ann Irvin was Ann Gregg.

Chapter 29

A Final Extra Twist

The story should have ended there, but there was one final twist in the tale.

While I was researching Ann's children, I discovered 2 possible Peter Hutchinson's. One born in 1784, who was a blacksmith at Dearham; (mentioned in the petition for clemency for Jane and Mary Ann Hutchinson) the other born in 1785, who was a basket maker.

Using the DNA results from descendants of both Peters and comparing the strength of the matches to other known Hutchinson descendants, showed that Peter the blacksmith was the son of William and Ann. This meant that Peter the basket maker who also matched but at a reduced level, must be William's nephew, and therefore not related to Ann Irvin. His grandfather and William's father were the same person, so Hutchinson DNA would be passed down both lines, but Ann's DNA only passed down through Peter the blacksmith's.

The three children born in the compter were Ann's children, not Williams, and as so, they should have no matches to Hutchinson DNA. Yet, there were matches between Peter the basket maker's descendants and those from all three groups. This meant that they all had Hutchinson genes, so William must have been the father.

Somehow, William had travelled the length of England from Cumberland to London and made his wife pregnant, so that she could avoid transportation! They must have developed a plan for Ann to give the children the surname Irving, which would become her final alias after her release, giving her a new identity and a clean slate. I'm currently trying to prove that Ann's mother was an Irving, showing Ann had used her mothers maiden name.

The final piece of the puzzle was where and when did Ann Gregg alias Hutchinson alias Irvin alias &c. &c, die?

After months of searching, I finally found her. She had passed away on February 15th 1848. Her age on the death certificate is shown as 81. However, based on her baptismal record my calculation is that she would have been 92 years old. She is shown on the death certificate as Widow of William Hutchinson, Basket Maker, Seaton, and died at the home of William Watson from Influenza. I tried to find the burial plot where Ann lay, but unfortunately a fire in 2006 destroyed all records of burial plots. Ann had managed to elude me one final time.

This great genealogical adventure has not only uncovered one of the most notorious Cumberland female criminals of her time, along with her law-breaking family, it has also revealed what appears to be an amazing love story, too.

Ann Hutchinson's Death Certificate.

Acknowledgements

The front cover is taken from "The Watercress Girl" an etching by John Raphael Smith depicting a watercress hawker, which is held at the Yale Centre for British art. Dated 1780 this image gives a clear impression of the type and style of the dress, worn in that period by someone like Ann Gregg. This is corroborated by newspaper descriptions of her.

The rear cover is taken from the Ordinance Survey may of Carlisle dated 1865. Although this is after the period when Ann Gregg was incarcerated there, The plan shown of the County gaol is exactly the same as it was during the period she spent there.

Books referred to in my research :-
The discoveries of John Poulter alias Baxter, by John Poulter.
Crime and society in England, 1750 - 1900 by Clive Emsley.
Rogues, Thieves an the Rule of Law 1718 - 1800 by Gwenda Morgan and Peter Rushton.
The State of the Prisons in England and Wales, (1779) by John Howard.

Other sources :-
Many web sites were visited and read in the course of my research, particularly sites referring to the "Transportation of Convicts", "English Criminal History", and "Crime and Punishment".
I have tried to investigate if any of this material is copyright, but unfortunately was not able to do so. If any writer believes that their copyright was infringed, please contact this author.

Archives

Archives were an invaluable resource of historical documents. In particular :-
Cumbria County Council Archive Services at Carlisle. Whitehaven and Kendal.
The National Archives, London.
London Metropolitan Archives.
Tyne and Wear Archives, Newcastle.
New South Wales Archives, Australia
The British Newspaper Archive.

DNA

DNA is now a vitally important element in genealogical research. Without DNA, it would have been impossible to research, prove and write this book.
There are several companies offering autosomal DNA tests, receiving your results is just the beginning of your journey.
I highly recommend the following two web sites, which were both invaluable to me. Amazingly they are both free.

GEDmatch was started in 2010 in response to the explosion of new DNA matches that were becoming available thanks to the use of autosomal DNA. A few tools were personally developed. The tools were so good we wanted to share them with other family genealogy researchers. The first such tool was computer matching of family trees. GEDmatch is a free site and its purpose continues to be to make advanced genealogy tools free to fellow genealogists.

DNA Painter is a website for chromosome mapping, allowing you to visualise and make notes on your DNA matches.

My sincere thanks to both of these web sites

Cumbria Archive Services

It would have been impossible to uncover Ann Gregg's story, and write this book without the help of Cumbria Archive Services. There are literally millions of documents in the archive just waiting to be read. This would be a daunting task without the help of the wonderful staff there.

Their help in suggesting where and how to start looking. Their patience producing records from within the archive, sometimes many times over. Their knowledge of local history and what the archives holds, helped me immensely. But most importantly, the gave me a new found love of local history.

If you are interested in family or local history, I highly recommend their services.

Cumbria Archive Service has existed since 1962 and has gathered together much of the surviving documentary heritage of the county of Cumbria for public access. Cumbria's archives provide a unique, exciting and inspiring resource that highlights why Cumbria is such a special place. Archives are profoundly important for learning. The archives are Cumbria's collective memory, providing authoritative evidence to help people solve problems and find out the truth. The Archive Service operates through four archive centres which are open to the public in Barrow, Carlisle, Kendal and Whitehaven.

County Council

The Story Tree

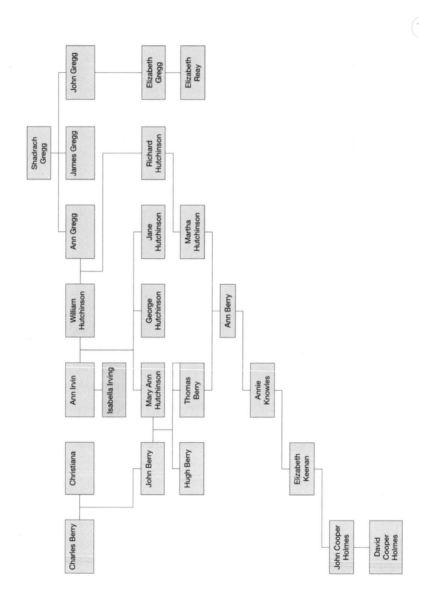